A. S. H

About the author of

The Renewing Gospel

Walter Russell Bowie, rector of Grace Church in New York City, was born in Virginia. He studied for the ministry at the Theological Seminary in Virginia, at Alexandria and at Union Theological Seminary, New York. Before coming to New York he was rector of St. Paul's Church in Richmond and editor of "The Southern Churchman." He is the author of numerous books, among the most popular being:

ON BEING ALIVE

THE MASTER: *A Life of Jesus Christ*

THE STORY OF THE BIBLE

THE INESCAPABLE CHRIST

SOME OPEN WAYS TO GOD

THE RENEWING GOSPEL

BY WALTER RUSSELL BOWIE

THE RENEWING GOSPEL

THE STORY OF THE BIBLE

ON BEING ALIVE

WHEN CHRIST PASSES BY

THE MASTER:
    A LIFE OF JESUS CHRIST

WHEN JESUS WAS BORN

THE INESCAPABLE CHRIST

SOME OPEN WAYS TO GOD

CHIMES AND THE CHILDREN

THE ARMOR OF YOUTH

THE ROAD OF THE STAR

SUNNY WINDOWS

THE MASTER OF THE HILL

THE CHILDREN'S YEAR

THE YALE LECTURES ON PREACHING

The

Renewing Gospel

Walter Russell Bowie

CHARLES SCRIBNER'S SONS

NEW YORK · LONDON

1935

TO

EMILY HAMILTON WELCH

JOYOUS IN WELL-BEING
FEARLESS IN ADVERSITY
UNRECKONING IN FRIENDSHIP

WITH GRATITUDE FOR HOSPITALITY THROUGH MANY
SUMMERS AT THE LITTLE NEW ENGLAND LAKE WHERE
THIS AND OTHER BOOKS WERE MAINLY WRITTEN

FOREWORD

The title of this book should make its purpose reasonably plain. We do not need a new gospel, though there be plenty of propagandists for this and that who think so; what we do need is an understanding of how endlessly an old gospel can reveal its new significance for us. The meaning of God as expressed in Christ ought forever to be blossoming into surer beliefs and a more sensitive expression of them, into a clearer conception of what would constitute a Christian life for individuals and for society, and into stronger effort to achieve that life. Thus though the Christian inheritance is old, every generation ought to produce men and women who in imagination, in purpose, and in power are Christians of a new kind. And the message that this can be so is what I mean by *The Renewing Gospel*.

The book is an expansion of the Lyman Beecher Lectures on Preaching, delivered at the Divinity School of Yale University in April, 1935. When the invitation to prepare and deliver these lectures first came to me through Dean Weigle, I wrote him to say that instead of writing lectures on sermon construction or technique I should like to try the harder task of working out, so far as I might be able, the interpretation of the gospel which the Christian preacher must needs be preaching in this present time. Of how large and adventurous a matter that was, I became increasingly aware as the preparation of the book went forward; but I am sure that it should be attempted. For the business of men in Christian pulpits today is not merely to produce interesting sermons on scattered themes; it is nothing less than to re-state the rich content of Christian thinking, and to illumine the ends of Christian conduct, until these become vital and kindling for our contemporary world. Whoever tries to do this will know how far short he falls of success; but this particular book will serve at least one purpose if it provokes its readers to search their own thoughts concerning the great matters with which it has made bold to deal.

The chapters which follow have been so rewritten and enlarged that those who heard the lectures at Yale will recognize them only partially. Yet it was only because the lectures were given that the book is written; and in this preface I want to thank the authorities of the Yale Divinity School for the invitation which I had to try to answer. And particularly I am grateful to Professor Henry Hallam Tweedy, who in Dean Weigle's absence abroad made himself my host; and to the other members of the Divinity School faculty, the students of the School and the visitors of Convocation Week, who gave to the lectures and the lecturer their generous welcome.

Finally, I would acknowledge the helpful counsel of those who have read parts of the manuscript and have made it better than it might otherwise have been by their suggestions:—the Dean of the General Theological Seminary, Hughell E. W. Fosbroke, and Professor Burton S. Easton; the Right Reverend Julius W. Atwood; E. Felix Kloman and Theodore P. Ferris, my colleagues at Grace Church; and Jean Bowie Evans.

And above all am I indebted to the indefatigable and devoted co-operation of my secretary, Miss Bertha M. Garvin, without whom this book could not have been completed.   WALTER RUSSELL BOWIE.

GRACE CHURCH RECTORY,
June 3, 1935.

CONTENTS

THE RENEWING GOSPEL

CHAPTER I

THE PREACHER AND THE PEOPLE

ONE of the distinguished contemporary figures in the public life of New England, ex-Governor John Gilbert Winant of New Hampshire, recounts that once when he was campaigning for the governorship, he was to address a gathering of citizens at a village grocery store. When he arrived, there was no gathering. In addition to the storekeeper, the one citizen in evidence was an old man sitting on a cracker-box. The storekeeper, thinking it incumbent on him to rally the only audience in sight, went over to the old man and said, as he indicated Mr. Winant, "This is the candidate for Governor." The old man looked up, stared, and then said slowly, "Well, I guess there'll be others."

In the long succession of books which deal with preaching, multitudinously there have been and there will be others. What significance therefore can any new venture upon this theme possess? Must not the subject be already in process of exhaustion?

So one might be inclined to think.

But then we turn and remember another fact. Still as in other decades men are preaching, and the people

come to listen. Here in one place every Sunday there
are a few. There in that other place are hundreds.
Yonder, in some great church where sounds a greater
voice, there are thousands. Added all together, it is
a very great multitude which every week comes to hear
what preachers will have to say. This is not accident.
It is not the passing whim that ripples over the surface
of men's interest and is gone. It is the stirring of something that issues from the deeps of human souls like the
stirring of the tides that come from the profundity of
the sea. In the meeting of the preacher and those who
come to hear him preach there is an influence which is
cosmic, and which has in it something as inevitable for
the life of the spirit as the attraction of the planets is
inevitable in the world of space. In the long run, men
preach because they are moved by a sense of something
infinite, and men and women come to listen because it
is of the infinite that they want to know. They want to
be made a little more aware of life and of what it leads
to. They want to find well-springs of water which do
not break through the dusty ground of the uninspired
day. They want to see the meaning of themselves and
of their world revealed in the light that never was on
land or sea; and they keep on believing, sometimes piti-
fully, and yet with patience and persistence, that somehow the preacher can tell them of these things.

That is why the subject of preaching is never out-
grown, and that is why it is never stale. What ought

2

men to be saying in this living time? To all those who are looking for what they know they lack, this is a subject as inexhaustible as the realities of life itself.

Now a book on preaching is obviously designed first for the interest of those who are to preach; but as we have already observed, the very fact of a preacher implies those he preaches to. Therefore all that we shall go on to think and to say should concern not only the man in the pulpit but equally the man in the pew. Certainly the congregation has a stake in what the preacher thinks about his work and in what he wants to make his message. So it is to no limited and professional class that our consideration will be directed. We shall be thinking of truths which one man may voice, but which a whole congregation of people must share if they are to be deeply real.

Beginning, however, with the figure of the preacher, what is he?

He is an individual fortified by a great fellowship and overshadowed by God.

He is an individual. Let every man who ascends the stairs of every great or humble pulpit, and let every man who is looking forward to becoming some day a preacher, remember the full implications of that. If there is any reality in the man at all, he is different from all other men. He is no sedulous ape to some one else. He is himself, and his business is to bring such a message about man and life and God as he, in his own honest experience, is discovering.

This truth ought to be set in the very forefront of our thinking, because to forget it is a tragedy. The failures in preaching come most often not because men lack brilliant gifts, but because they bring nothing that seems intimately and intensely true. <u>What hungry souls want is bread, the home-made bread which has been baked in the oven of the convictions of a man's own soul.</u> When preachers do bring this, then their work is great, whether or not their names are ever blazoned in the newspapers. Many a congregation goes to hear a preacher year in and year out without any thought of being attracted by some more glittering orator across the street. They do so because they feel that this man is not blown about by every passing breeze. He is not echoing popular opinion. He is trying to tell what he himself in all honesty has felt and thought. Instinctively they feel concerning him what old George Herbert put in his clear words:

> "How happy is he born or taught
>   That serveth not another's will,
> Whose armour is his honest thought,
>   And simple truth his utmost skill!" [1]

This does not mean, of course, that the preacher ought to try to be different for the sake of being different. On the contrary, he is not to try to be anything

[1] *The Character of a Happy Life*, by Sir Henry Wotton.

but himself. And if he is himself, the real self which God is ready to release, then he will not be peculiar nor given to any cheap self-display, but he will have the distinction of a personality that humbly accepts and reverently uses the particular thing which God has seen fit to create in him. There is noble truth in the words which George Eliot put into the mouth of the great artificer of violins:

> " 'Tis God gives skill,
> But not without men's hands: He could not make
> Antonio Stradivari's violins
> Without Antonio." [2]

He might make other violins, and conceivably other violins as good; but without Stradivarius, God himself could not make the violins which Stradivarius made. So the divine impulse may get itself expressed in many sermons; but every individual preacher can remember that there is something he has to say, and a way in which he may learn to say it, which no other servant of the Most High can duplicate.

Of course it is sometimes hard for a man who wants to keep his spirit simple and modest to believe this. A young man, particularly, who is looking forward to the ministry or who is just entering upon it shrinks from assuming that he has anything notable to give. He thinks that if he were a great figure he could then be confident; but he feels that he is not great. In the

[2] *Stradivarius*, by George Eliot, l. 151.

entrance hall to the building at Harvard College which bears the name of Phillips Brooks is a bronze tablet with a noble inscription in memory of that great preacher. It speaks of him as "majestic in stature, impetuous in utterance, rejoicing in the truth," and goes on to say that "he brought by his life and doctrine fresh faith to a people, fresh meaning to ancient creeds." But the average man feels that no one of these things is true of him. He is not "majestic in stature," either in body or mind, but rather one who seems in his own estimation to be level with the crowd. He may not be "impetuous in utterance," but may instead stumble much when he tries to speak. He may want to be as one who is "rejoicing in the truth"; but, though he loves truth, he may know that often he gropes uncertainly as he tries to find it. Nevertheless, it is true that many a man by his own faithful living, and by his steady and honest witness to the convictions which life is teaching him day by day, will in ways far beyond his knowing bring "fresh faith to a people," and "fresh meaning to ancient creeds."

It is not by any means only the men who stand in conspicuous places who have left their strong and individual impress upon other men and upon the spiritual values of their time. Back of the great Phillips Brooks there stood, among others, a professor of whom most of the world had never heard, Doctor William Sparrow, Dean of the Virginia Seminary, whose motto was,

"Seek the truth, come whence it may, cost what it will."
And it was of him that Phillips Brooks wrote: "Upon
the whole he is one of the three or four men whom I
have known whom I look upon with perpetual gratitude
for the help and direction which they have given to my
life." [3] In the nave of Westminster Abbey is buried the
body of David Livingstone, missionary, explorer, and
creator in many ways of a new life for the continent
of Africa; but back of this great figure there stood an
old Sunday School teacher, David Hogg, in the little
village of Blantyre in Scotland, who inspired Livingstone as a boy, and who on his death-bed said to David
Livingstone, "Now, lad, make religion the everyday
business of your life and not a thing of fits and starts." [4]

In a volume of the delightful essays of the late
Samuel McChord Crothers, there is one in which he
describes the lectures supposed to have been given in
a theological seminary by a retired colonel who had
been added to its faculty. Speaking to his young students for the ministry, he said, "I have often noticed
the way in which the members of your profession interpret the call of duty to what they speak of as 'a larger
field of usefulness.' I have no reason to doubt their
disinterestedness, but I have been often amazed at what
they called a larger field. Frequently they will evacuate

[3] *Life and Letters of Phillips Brooks,* by Alexander V. G. Allen,
Vol. I, p. 311.
[4] *Personal Life of David Livingstone,* by W. Garden Blaikie,
p. 33.

a strategic point, leaving an important part of the field open to the enemy, and retire to a position of no importance for offensive operations. I could not understand the movement till it was explained to me that they are accustomed to use the word 'field' in an agricultural rather than in a military sense. They are thinking of a field fenced in and under pastoral care; they are not thinking of it as a field of battle, where a lonely hilltop may be the key to the situation." [5]

But the fact is that the key to the situation may indeed be the lonely hilltop; and many a man, working out his ministry in what seems an inconspicuous place, if he honors his individual responsibility and brings to it the utmost he has, may know that he is rendering service which is vital to the whole battle-line of the Kingdom of God.

Edward Thring, headmaster of Uppingham School in the mid-nineteenth century, took what was an obscure institution and made it into one of the great educational influences of England. In his early ministry it was remarked that "nothing seemed small to him"; and one of his fellow-workers wrote: "I do not believe he would have neglected a school lesson for the chance of becoming an archbishop. I do not believe he would have omitted one portion of the day's routine, if that omission had injured a single boy, for the position of highest

[5] *Among Friends,* p. 200. I have taken the liberty of reversing the order of the two clauses in the last sentence of Doctor Crothers' paragraph.—W. R. B.

eminence his country could bestow." And Thring himself set down one day in his journal these words that throw a revealing light upon the secret of his greatness: "How strange life is. How little one knows what is best! Life is best, the living the day manfully, truly and humbly. Not what we plan, but how we live. Not what we aim at doing, but how we do what we have to do—that is God's life." [6]

Let the preacher remember, then, first of all that he is an individual, commissioned to his particular task, with all the unique incentive which that brings. Then he will go on to remember also that *he is an individual fortified by a great fellowship.*

It is by the fellowship that the particular man in the pulpit is strengthened and corrected. By the sense of fellowship his individuality will be kept from falling into idiosyncrasies. He is a particular person and a different one. But it is not his business to express peculiarity. He is to try from the angle of his own knowledge and understanding to interpret a truth which belongs not to himself but to mankind.

There is a fellowship with those who have gone before. Every Christian preacher will be a better man and a better messenger if he cultivates an historic imagination. One of the values of those communions which stress the thought of the historic continuity is that they

[6] *Life and Letters of Edward Thring,* by George R. Parkin, pp. 497, 498, 366.

help men to do this. It gives a noble dignity to a man's whole sense of his vocation when he remembers that he, however unworthy, belongs to an august succession. What he is endeavoring to do Augustine and Chrysostom did, and Bernard of Clairvaux, and Wyclif, and Hugh Latimer, and John Robinson, and many another prophetic voice of the more recent years. Because he too is called by their great desire and in spirit is made one with these, something of the greatness of their ambassadorship clothes him too.

Now it is true that there is a contemporary mood which is impatient of the examples and the patterns of the past. Many today insist that life must be an immediate and personal experience and not be suffered to become a hollow parade of second-hand attempts to repeat in changing times the ideas of ancient yesterdays. But though a life must flame to its vital expression through our own selves and in our present moment, nevertheless the present moment can have no great value unless it is linked to the past, and becomes itself a link binding the future to that past. All great meanings grow out of long developments. Even a moving picture film, treated discontinuously, would become absurd. Cut a film into its tiny separate pictures, and let one of them shine by itself upon the screen. It expresses life and action in one particular instant. There will be the figures in the exact attitudes and postures in which, at a particular second of time, they were caught; but the picture by itself will be grotesque and ridiculous. Only when that picture begins to flow into others, so that the half-complete actions and movements go on into their intelligible completeness, does the picture become a sensible and fascinating thing. How much more does the same truth hold for the mighty fact of life! No single moment of it has significance by itself. It is a part of the immemorial pageant of the ages; part of the long story of the human soul which is lifted into dignity and noble interest only when we begin to feel it as a whole.

With our little experience, our scraps of ideas, and our isolated notions, we turn and contemplate the august sweep of human life. The light of God has fallen upon it through many generations. "I believe in the Communion of Saints," men say as they recite the creed; and in the *Te Deum* they sing, "The glorious company of the Apostles, the goodly fellowship of the Prophets, the noble army of Martyrs; praise thee. The holy Church throughout all the world doth acknowledge thee." At the music of those sonorous words long vistas of spiritual history begin to open. This civilization of ours and all that it contains are no sudden creation. They have been fashioned for us by the mighty spirits who have dreamed and desired, dared, endured, suffered perhaps, and sacrificed, and won those achievements which are ours now, because they first were theirs. Paul passing like a flame across the Roman world until the fire of his spirit seemed to be quenched at last in a Roman prison, yet even in his dying rising again to shine like a star of heroic truth before the eyes of man forever; Francis of Assisi bringing the sweetness of Jesus back to a world from which his figure seemed long since to have departed; John Huss going unshaken to his martyr's death at Constance; Savonarola in the Duomo with Florence awed and eager at his feet; Martin Luther riding on to Worms to confront an emperor in his lonely loyalty to a new and impassioned conviction of his Master's truth; John Wesley rising in conventional and complacent England of the eighteenth century to bring again the gospel to the poor; Robertson and Bushnell and Brooks revealing in modern times the everlasting glory of the gospel: these are the figures whose strength and beauty are wrought into whatever inheritance of nobility we are aware of in our souls.

Nor is it only the victorious figures who have made life significant. There is something infinitely touching and purifying to our emotions in the thought of the long struggle of life in the common crowd: life with its baseness as well as its beauty; life with its mud and slime as well as with its mountain peaks of snow; life with the pall of its evil shot through forever by the gleams of its higher hope and its unquenchable desires. In the shadow of the choir of St. Paul's Cathedral, there at the teeming heart of London, stands a monument to mark where from 1116 to 1613 the old St. Paul's cross used to be. The inscription on it says that the new cross has been raised to commemorate the ancient cross "whereat amid such scenes of good and evil as make up human affairs the conscience of Church and Nation through five centuries found public utterance." That conscience which there found utterance was a stumbling and groping thing. From the foot of the cross great preachers proclaimed the gospel; but there also Wyclif's first translation of the New Testament into English was burned. There edicts of Church and State which laid their heavy attempted bondage on men's minds were read; but there also spoke the voices of men who were to be the prophets and sometimes the martyrs of new and better days. There was revealed the complex of human nature wherein ignorance and grandeur are so strangely mingled, and there was shaped little by little that impulse of the suffering, sorrowing, blundering, striving human spirit which through the darkness and against the temptations that come to all has slowly cleared the pathway to those levels of achievement on which, if we choose, our life today may move.

The man who wishes to be a true and understanding preacher may well read history and deepen his sense of identity with all the long movement of the past; yet, of course, his fellowship is not only with the past but with the present also. It is with all living people, and especially with those actual men and women who make up his own congregation. The preacher's fellowship with his own congregation is suggested by the other and larger name which belongs to his profession. There are indeed various names by which he may be called, and the simplest and widest of them is best. He may be spoken of as the "Rector"; but that may have a stiff, official sound. He may be called a "Priest"—which name can be noble if it does not result in exalting the man's own importance, but rather makes him conscious that he is meant to be a mediator between God and all the people. He may be called "Father"; and in some communions that title has become familiar and natural, and in some other communions there is busy effort to bring it in. In France during the World War a certain very young Episcopal clergyman met the quick and delightful Henry Sloane Coffin, and said to him, "Would you mind calling me 'Father so and so'?" "Oh, no," said Doctor Coffin, "I will call you 'Grandfather' if it will make you feel any better." But "Father" this and that, even though it make some feel better, is not the ultimate word. Neither is "Pastor," though that word has gracious values too. The final word, and the inclusive word, is "Minister." It is as a *servant* in his Master's name that a man has a right to be a preacher. He can be no true preacher unless he is a *minister* first. Now and then we hear the wish expressed that there might be in the Church a group of men trained only for preaching, and giving all their time and energy to that. It is upon the surface an alluring thought; but it does not develop into fact, and one doubts whether it ever will, or could, or ought to do so. In the long run, men cannot preach unless they are in touch with people. They must go in and out, trying to serve, to help, to understand, for only so can their preaching be kept from becoming academic, and be instead the interpretation of realities which they have learned in the midst of the human group.

Happy and blessed is the man who goes forward into the wondering expression of those friendships which his ministry holds out to him. He will be touching people sometimes at the level of their worst and often at the level of their best, but always—when these contacts are genuine—in aspects of their souls which are intensely real. He can see human beings who have dropped the masks which so often in their shyness or their self-consciousness or in their shame they wear. His associations are not built on some partial aspect of their being. His friendships are not made merely out of acquaintance on the golf links or partnership at a bridge table or association in a business venture. They are deeper even than mutual tastes and æsthetic sympathies which bring many men and women together in their pleasures or in their artistic appreciations. His friendships are built on that basis which is deepest of all, the fundamental desire of the human soul to find itself in

God. Many a minister can name over in his mind the friendships which he cherishes as the most beautiful heritage of the years, friendships with men whom he may not see for long intervals but whose unchanging comradeship he knows. When he sees them again he does not have to reach out tentatively for new contacts. He does not have to wonder whether old tastes and sympathies have changed. He knows where those others are and what they are; and when he meets with them, they meet immediately as pilgrims on a familiar road where the face of each one is lighted alike by those hopes and desires which stream from the sky of the consciousness of God. Every minister who is alive to his infinite opportunities of building friendships is creating new friendships like that today. If he is not doing so, then there is something wrong with his own soul, or there is a barrier somewhere between him and his people.

But there is one thing which those to whom the minister might be a friend should always remember: namely, that perfect friendship must grow out of mutual desire. The minister cannot force his way into the secret citadel of another human personality. He cannot batter in the door of a man's or woman's heart. He cannot indelicately knock for admission into confidences unless there is welcome from within. When there is welcome, then men and women understand what the relationship between a minister and the souls of his congregation can become. There are those who know that the voice

16

of the one whom they have trusted as an interpreter of God can reach through to them in hours of sickness when other voices, even of those very near and dear, may fail to penetrate, bringing a quietness and confidence that flow through all the faintness of their minds; until presently they are lifted by tides of strength and recovery which medicine alone could not release. There are some who know what a minister can mean to them when they are in a hospital dreading the operation which is about to come; know that he can help to steady them, to banish fear, and transmit a strange sense of peace which comes not from him but *through* him as the gift of God; and they know that what he does for them may minimize shock, and not only tranquillize the spirit but help the body more quickly to get well. There are those also who know that the minister can bring comfort and light to men and women who may be very near the hour of death, so that without distress they may feel the bark of their existence moving with the tide which bears them out to sea; and they know that at the last he can help them lift their eyes and find their faces lighted by the vision of Him whom the disciples saw walking toward them through the darkness and the peril on the waters of the lake of Galilee.

But the preacher must have more than these two realities of which we have already thought. He must be not only *an individual fortified by a great fellowship*.

He must be such an one overshadowed also by God.

I can never forget the day, now many years ago, when for the first and only time I saw Mount Rainier. I was on a train that skirted the level shores of Puget Sound. Near at hand the foreground was flat and uninspiring; but as I looked to the east, suddenly I saw a white radiance shining in the sky. Above the range of lesser mountains, above a drifting bank of cloud, the glittering snow-capped cone of the great mountain lifted itself, majestic and alone, against the sky. So great it seemed, and so unearthly, that for one breath-taking moment of surprise it was difficult to believe that it was anything more than a mirage of sunlight and of mist. But as I looked again, I knew that it was real, and the whole landscape assumed an instant dignity because of that transcendent beauty brooding there.

In some such way, men lift their eyes from the low coast line of our ordinary life, and desire to see the greatness of God. They wish to believe that above all lesser things his greatness and his beauty stand. They want to feel that the horizons are not flat or empty, but that the Eternal is there, lifted above the levels of our time.

That hunger for God is the reflection in living men of the same deep longing by which souls in every generation have been moved, and to which they have given expression in their own instinctive ways. In the early centuries when monasticism was just beginning, a

18

huntsman whose pack had led him far afield encoun-
tered the hermit Macedonius and said to him, "What
are you doing in this barren spot?" "I too am a huntsman," was the answer; "I am hunting for my God, and
yearn to capture and enjoy Him. Him I desire to see,
and never will I rest from this my gallant hunting."
And another of his contemporaries wrote: "This is a
thing that every one ought to know—that we have eyes
within, deeper than these eyes; and a hearing deeper
than this hearing. As the eyes of sense behold and
recognize the face of a friend or loved one, so the eyes
of the true and faithful soul, spiritually illuminated with
the light of God, behold and recognize the true Friend.
. . . The soul is smitten with passionate love for God,
and so directed into all virtues by the Spirit. It possesses an unbounded, unfailing love for the Lord for
Whom it longs." [7]

In every time men are looking for some other man
who will bring them a surer sense of God. Unless a
preacher can bring that, his utterance will be clanging
brass and a tinkling cymbal. He will be a mechanical
echo of the shallow jargon of his time. But if his soul
has dwelt within the over-shadowing realities of God,
and if he speaks as a man whom God has possessed,
then in a strange and moving way he becomes authoritative. He has a message which will break through

[7] *The Vision of God,* by H. E. Kirk, p. 193. Used by permission
of Longmans, Green & Co.

him in spite of everything. He is the spokesman of convictions too urgent to be denied.

The pages of the Bible are starred with the great figures of those who had on their souls something tremendous which they had to say, and so were irresistible. Moses declared of himself that he was "slow of speech and of a stammering tongue"; but when the oppression of his people stirred the passion in his heart, his message blazed so that Pharaoh shrank before it. Elijah the Tishbite, lonely but intrepid, confronted Ahab the king with the terrible moral truthfulness which left Ahab naked and defenceless. Amos, the shepherd of Tekoa, outraged at the sight of flaunted evil, launched his prophetic judgments before which priest and people trembled. And in the later time, John the Baptist showed again the power of the man, unadorned though he may be with outward trappings, whose words come out like living sparks from the fire of conviction burning in his soul.

The Fourth Gospel may not be meticulous history, but it does give great pictures of the souls of men; and according to this Gospel, when men asked John the Baptist, "What sayest thou of thyself?" this is what he answered: "I am a voice!" Mark the proud significance of that. Perhaps at first we do not mark it. A voice, we say,—what is that to boast of? The world is full of voices. No, but it is not. Not in any such sense as John dared to proclaim himself to be one. The world is full of little whisperings, a confused chatter of this and that, ejaculations shrill and inconsistent, falsettos and discord and confusion. Only here and there out of the blur and medley rises the great note of the authentic voice. When Caruso sang, the blind might know when he appeared. They did not need to see. Over the chorus of lesser men and women, the great voice floated, vibrant, triumphant, unmistakable. So it is in the moral and religious sphere. Over the crowd-clamor, over the ineffective utterance of the unsure souls fumbling for expression, rings the message of some high spirit who knows what he would say. For him the meaning of life is clear. Its details are swept like notes into the mightier harmony. When he speaks, men stand in hushed astonishment. When he speaks, it is as though the trumpet blew.

"I am the voice of one crying in the wilderness," said this same John. Consider the superb disdain of that. He did not go to city and town, but city and town came to him. He did not run after the multitude and fawn upon them with persuasion. He stood still in the majestic confidence of his moral certitude, and the multitude beat a path through the wilderness to where he was. So is it ever with a great voice. Men imagine that they must curry favor before they will be heard. They must try by all sorts of devious means to gain what they call influence, in order that, being influential, they may then be listened to. But it is not so with the ultimate authority. Let a man find his own place first. Let him nourish his own convictions in solitary self-communion, as John did. Let him dream his mighty dreams, search the depths of his own heart, and scan the stars that march above him in the sky of the thoughts of God, and then in no petty accents, but out of his own clear, unfettered freedom let him speak. John spent the years of his preparation, went through the slow process of his soul's maturing, there in the wilderness of Judæa. So did Amos long before. So did Elijah. Jesus dwelt as a lad in little Nazareth. He began his ministry by the quiet waters of the lake of Galilee. He did not go first to the great city. He would not be moulded by the conventionality of the crowd. First of all, he possessed himself, in order that afterward he might possess and master men. The One who was to come and the prophet who proclaimed him, were alike in this. They fashioned their utterance not before any sounding-board of the vainly sought approval and applause of men. They fashioned it rather before the awful wideness of the solitudes of God. Therefore, when they spoke, infinity spoke through them. "A voice crying in the wilderness," and behold the world was full of the sound thereof!

"Ah, but those are the great men and the great moments," the preacher of today may say. "I cannot speak with ringing certitude like theirs. I am bold today, and timorous tomorrow."

Well, so were most of the great ones also. They too had their hours of inspiration, and their hours of inability. "The spirit bloweth and is still." But there is no defeat in that. Danger lies rather in the idea that because a man is not *always* prevailing, he can *never* be prevailing. And still more danger would be in the notion that the minister and preacher is a sort of spiritual superman, immune to ordinary doubts and fears. His honest limitations may be his strength.

Too often people suppose that the minister must have a dogmatic certainty about every aspect of a conquering faith, and that he may be embarrassed not to meet this expectation. Men and women are shy of going to a minister with their perplexities because they say, "It must all be so clear to him that he would not understand." Or they visit upon the minister that most damaging of all suppositions, which shows either that they have never tried to approach him simply or else that he by some pomposity has defeated their approach—the supposition that "he would be shocked." As a matter of fact, every minister has his hours when he must grapple with doubt, as all real men and women do. He too will walk on roads where fogs roll in from an empty sea and the mountain tops are hidden. He too will often wrestle in agony through the darkness with some unseen antagonist of frustration and inner despair; and blessed is he if like Jacob wrestling with the angel by Peniel he nevertheless says on behalf of his own soul and the soul of his people, "I will not let thee go except thou bless me!" It is in his wrestlings, his real wrestlings with the same perplexities and contradictions by which all men and women sometimes are distressed, that the true minister gains such power as he may have to unlock the secrets of other human hearts. For through these things he will be going forward, by the grace of God, toward possession of the Reality which will grow clearer and more beautiful as his experience grows; and he will be learning, as it is his business to try to do, to put the living truths into expression. His preaching will rise to its greatest heights not when he seems to be saying some new thing, not when he astonishes the congregation with some so-called original idea, or holds them spell-bound for the moment by the colors of his rhetoric. His power will be not even when he seems to speak that which his hearers will feel is truth, but truth of a sort which had never occurred to them before. No, the most vital preaching rather is when men and women, hearing what is said, go away saying to themselves, "I know that must be true because I have somehow always felt it. He said today what I have always believed, only I could never quite put it into words."

Thus far we have been thinking mainly of the preacher, and of what he ought to be. But we remembered at the outset that he is nothing, except in a relationship. He preaches to living men and women who because of their own reasons desire to be preached to. And why? What do people want the message of the preacher for?

In the first place, they want to be helped to feel that life makes sense.

So much of modern existence is disjointed and disintegrating. The mechanical noise and hurry in which men live makes it difficult for the soul to stand still and see things in perspective. Even to cross a street, they must start nervously and be alert to dodge accidental danger. Life in general may seem to be like the city's traffic—a confusion of restless energies twisting this way and that, a mêlée into which men plunge in the morning as they go to work and from which they emerge tired in the afternoon, with no clear consciousness that anything significant has happened in the hours between. "Is this all that existence is?" they ask—"clamor and commotion, and a routine that seems to be getting nowhere?" They hear pseudo-philosophers answer yes. They hear many modern prophets of a mechanistic science say that the universe itself is nothing but a congeries of accidental atoms, and that man is no more than a restless pygmy gesticulating a moment on the surface of a tiny planet on which the great stars look indifferently down. He hears that; but an instinct deep within him rises to deny it. Somehow he believes that his insatiable quest for meaning in his universe

will not be met with ultimate contempt. He is willing to
struggle, but he seeks to struggle for a purpose. It has
been truly written: "Suffering is always bearable if it
can be understood as a part of a process having a dis-
cernible end. What is insufferable to man is that his
self-conscious existence should challenge the universe
for a brief moment without being able to relate itself
organically to it." [8]

When men and women come to hear a preacher, what
they most deeply want—whether or not explicitly they
put it into words—is assurance that life does "relate
itself organically" to a universal meaning. They want
to believe that all the fragmentary concerns of every
day come together in the dignity of some great interpretation. They may not expect the preacher to tell them
exactly how. They are not asking of him some gigantic
feat of intellectual synthesis. But they trust that he will
make them feel that it is so. They will not depend only
on what he says. They will be seeking for a look in
his eyes, a sense of poise which he may give, an atmosphere around him as of one who has pioneered beyond
the dusty ways. They will hope that he will be as a man
upon a hilltop who turns back to them a shining face,
and cries the news that all the tangled forest paths do
lead into a highroad, and that ahead are great horizons
and the splendor of the rising sun.

For the preacher to do this, he must not merely

[8] *Reflections on the End of an Era,* by Reinhold Niebuhr, p. 196.

preach a sermon; he must in humility, but with relentless self-requirement, *be* a sermon. He must show that,
whatever be his limitations, he is at least trying to put
himself at the center of things, and to see life steadily
and to see it whole. Because he is "a man of God," and
takes time for meditation and for prayer (nor let him
dare to fail in this!), he ought to have about him a
quality which makes all the world he moves in more
significant. He is one who has tried to understand and
to interpret the worth of common things. He has listened for the heavenly harmony in the midst of this
world's distractions; and if that be so, then when he
speaks, though men may forget what he has said, they
will go away assured and steadied by something which
has sounded through his voice.

The second thing people want when they come to
hear a preacher is <u>instruction</u>.

That, of course, is not to say that they want to listen
to a pedagogue. They will have scant patience with a
conceited self-assurance which parades its own academic
ideas. But they will be equally impatient with windy
exhortations. They are looking for the man who will
tell them simply, truly, and explicitly of facts in the
realm of religion which they do not know, and which
he has been commissioned to study and to master. As
Albert Edward Day truly said in his notable Lyman
Beecher Lectures in 1934: "Only a genuine interest in

the people who attend our ministry and a vivid under-standing of their needs artificial and real, and of the conflicts into which those needs precipitate them, and of the deforming, mutilating, paralyzing effects of those conflicts, and of the spiritual therapy which can elim-inate those effects, and of the personal strategy which can give the real and fundamental needs some satisfy-ing answer—only this can make our preaching a real ministry to personality—a creation and re-creation of souls." [9]

The most characteristic modern preaching has taken its cue from the psychological approach. It is not deductive, but inductive. It does not begin with large religious doctrines and then bring these down to their particular applications. It begins with the living person, and his confused but vital impulses; and it explores the possibilities for these, until at last it shows the frustra-tion of the irreligious life, and reveals the great high-roads of religious faith as the way in which the man himself must choose to go when he has found the real direction of his soul. An authority in applied psychol-ogy, C. G. Jung, has written in his *Modern Man in Search of a Soul,* "Among all my patients in the second half of life—that is to say, over thirty-five—there has not been one whose problem in the last resort was not that of finding a religious outlook on life. It is safe to

[9] *Jesus and Human Personality,* by Albert Edward Day, p. 238. By permission of the Abingdon Press, copyright 1934.

say that every one of them fell ill because he had lost that which the living religions of every age have given to their followers, and none of them has been really healed who did not regain his religious outlook." [10]

The urgent opportunity of the preacher today is to know enough of psychology illumined by religion to help men and women understand themselves; and his glory will be to lift their understanding up to the light of the beauty which shines from God. The preacher who looks into human personalities with revealing eyes will see in every man a vein of finer sentiment like a virgin spring. The hard crust of conventionality may have formed over it and hidden it from sight. The dust of this world's arid business may have drifted into it and choked its flow. But still it is there, never wholly stifled, never buried so deep that it cannot be revealed. He will be forever exploring for this hidden fountain in the people to whom he preaches, and his human sympathy will be like a divining rod which makes him know where the answering waters are. He will know that under the surface of even the hardest man there is a well of tears; that no man is quite invulnerable to poignant memories, or to the stabbing suggestion of old sorrows or old joys; and that there is a chord of emotional understanding which if it is truly struck by one heart will set up its echoes everywhere.

But of course it is not only about themselves that

[10] *Modern Man in Search of a Soul,* by C. G. Jung, p. 264.

people want to be instructed. They want also to have a more intelligent knowledge of what the life of man historically has been, and what the forces creating history may be now.

That knowledge, of course, ought to include the Bible. It is a lamentable fact that people are so ignorant as many of them are of that immortal Book. Usually they will not read it for themselves, because they get confused in its labyrinthine differences. But if the preacher has studied his Bible as he ought to, until he sees with fresh imagination the everlasting figures in it, saints and sinners, good men and bad men and men half-good; watches how characters grow, and change their world, or are changed by it; traces the majestic moral forces by which both individuals and nations at length are judged—then such a preacher can give to his people a background of understanding against which their own thought is corrected. And of course the Bible is not the only record he will want to have at his command. Whatever he has read and knows of science, of other histories, of other religions, and of great men in any nation and of any time, will enrich his power to widen his people's sympathies, enlighten their prejudices, and develop in them that discrimination by which the timeless realities are understood.

Moreover, the congregation which has learned to trust the man who preaches to them will want enlightenment on the forces which are shaping personal and social destinies today. What is the Christian way ahead in economics, in politics, in international relations? The man in the pulpit is not a technician, but he is a teacher; and a congregation of earnest people ought not to excuse him if, through timidity or through lazy ignorance, he has no word of living counsel in the name of God. Of course there are innumerable pitfalls of hasty or half-informed utterance into which the preacher may stumble; but the presence of pitfalls cannot justify a moral cowardice which refuses responsible leadership along an urgent road. The preacher will not try to instruct sociologists or business men or statesmen about the details of difficulties which they know better than he; but he will insist on furnishing for his people searchlights of moral and spiritual evaluation by which every immediate policy shall be judged and the distant goals of worth-while purpose be made plain. Representative church assemblies have increasingly been doing just this thing. They have spoken with prophetic clearness and prophetic courage. They have rebuked in the name of Christ old injustices which many church-members have been willing to tolerate, they have proclaimed the worth of human personality, and have championed specific social readjustments on behalf of the disadvantaged man. It is a revealing thing to see how many of the measures to which the United States have been driven in the present economic crisis, measures which subordinate the old unlimited license of in-

dividual profit to a new corporate responsibility and
co-operation, are those which for the last score of years
leaders in the Church have been proclaiming in the name
of the Kingdom of God. It is true that no specific
political or social program can be identified with the
gospel, and religion is not synonymous with any particular Recovery Act. Nevertheless the central message of
the Christian social gospel has been and will be vindicated by the inescapable facts of life. And it is the
business of the Christian preacher to have sufficient
knowledge and sufficient boldness to tell his people of
these things.

A further influence which a congregation wants is the
double one—according to changing times and changing
needs—of encouragement and of comfort. The preacher
at his best should be a mystic, unconsciously conveying
God, as Moses did, who "wist not that his face shone";
he should be a teacher, making clear the roads of right
thinking and right choice; but he should be something
also more than these. He must be the friend who not
only helps his people see their further duty, but who
gives them better heart for what they already have to
do, and sometimes also for what they have to bear.

Much of life is made up of routine. Once at the
Epiphany season a preacher spoke to his people on "The
Road of the Star," a sermon which had to do with the
lovely story of the Wise Men who followed their

heavenly sign on the long, romantic journey that led to the presence of Christ. After it a young mother came to him and said, "Often I should like to go on roads like that, and I cannot. There are Sundays when I want to come to church, and instead I have to stay at home and look after a sick child." Those words of hers made him understand how important it is that the loftiest religious themes must have their feet upon the earth; and on the next Sunday he tried to preach, as though for her, on "The Road of the Common Day." On that road most people are walking. They are busy about small matters. They are grappling with obscure temptations. They are going forward to tedious duties where there is no heroic drum-beat to which they can keep step. They are carrying on a small business where it is difficult sometimes even to be honest, and very difficult to keep any generous imagination of the human service it can represent. They are teaching a class of half-responsive children in a school. They are going through the daily round of sweeping floors, and dusting furniture, and providing meals, and making what might be a bare house into a home. In these things men and women need the message of religion as a friendly and intimate encouragement. If they cannot seem to go on romantic spiritual journeys seeking Christ, they need to know that Christ is already with them in whatever beauty of spirit they manifest in the ordinary things they do. Over their small post of duty the star of the meaning of God can shine as truly as it shone once over a stable in a little town; and it is the privilege of the preacher to make them see that this is so.

There are times also when people will need comfort. Not all the appliances of our modern civilization can act as a bulwark against the ultimate impact of suffering, bewilderment and loss. The noises of the radio cannot drown the question of the final mystery; the Ford car cannot take us out of reach of inexorable fact. Sometime the hearts of all men and women will be crying out for a gospel which helps them to look through loss to a conviction that dawns ahead, to find a faith which will be greater than despair, to trust in spite of every seeming contradiction that life at last is good. They will want to hear a man who not only by what he says, but by what he is, can bring them light in their dark hour.

Finally, men and women will desire from a preacher that he shall make them grow. If they have been listening to him week by week, they want to feel presently that something has happened; and that in this way and in that they are different from what they were a while before.

Roger Williams, pioneer of religious liberty in the American colonies of the early seventeenth century, was also a preacher who loved people and wanted to see religion bring forth in them its manifest fruits. He wrote a book to which he gave the ample title: *"Experiments of Spiritual Life and Health and their Preservatives. In which the weakest child of God may get assurance of his spiritual life and blessedness, and the strongest may find proportionable discoveries of his Christian growth and the cause of it."*

And thus he expressed his desire:

"My scope is to fill each Christian soul with rejoicing: I speak peace and joy to the weakest lamb and child (in Christianity). . . . To this poor weak one I speak peace and joy and say, this spiritual poverty is blessed and is the first step or round of that spiritual ladder, Matthew 5: Blessed are the poor in spirit, for theirs is the Kingdom of Heaven.

"Secondly, I sound joyful alarums of encouragement to the strong to grow (as Peter exhorteth) in the grace and knowledge of the Lord Jesus." [11]

Sometimes this growth that comes from preaching may be very gradual. It may show itself in the slow creation of a different intellectual climate. The glaciers of old religious fears and theological prejudices may have melted. Traditional loyalties are no longer frozen into old hard forms. The man who was once suspicious of any new ways of interpreting truth, hostile to biblical criticism, frightened at any re-examination of ancient creeds, may find that under preaching which he has grown to trust a whole new world of happier belief is

[11] *Roger Williams, Prophet and Pioneer,* by Emily Easton, p. 290.

blossoming in his mind and heart. Sometimes also he will find that his attitude toward life and the relative importance he attached to its different values and ambitions have changed in this same way. There was a sermon preached once in a country church, among the vestrymen of which was a certain vigorous and highly explosive gentleman who had recently lost a beautiful setter dog. The dog had been shot by the overseer of a neighboring estate, and great was the outburst of indignation. But the sermon was on forgiveness. It made the heart of this unwilling but honest listener uneasy. Going out of church, the first person he saw was the overseer. He marched straight up and confronted him. "Johnson," he said, "you shot my dog; but damn you, I forgive you!"

Not always will the preacher have such abrupt and unexpected results from his labors. Sometimes these will seem singularly empty and unfruitful. But nevertheless with a steady heart, and often with a happy heart, he can keep on. And even at his most difficult moments he can well remember what sturdy Martin Luther once said to a young theologian who found preaching a great burden: "Yes, my dear fellow, it was the same with me. I shrank from it just as you do; but I had to undertake it. I was forced to it, and I began in the refectory, before the brothers. Oh, how frightened I was! I had fifteen arguments with which I tried to persuade Doctor Staupitz, under this very pear-tree, to let me off, but that did no good. Finally, when I said, 'You are trying to kill me; I cannot live three months,' he replied: 'Very well, in God's name. The Lord has large affairs on hand, and needs wise men up yonder!' " [12]

[12] *Martin Luther, the Man and His Work,* by Arthur C. McGiffert, p. 49.

CHAPTER II

SOME BLAZES ON THE THEOLOGICAL TRAIL

I N the first chapter we were thinking of the two factors which manifestly are involved in all preaching: that is to say, the preacher himself on the one hand, and on the other hand the people. Ideally, he is to be an individual fortified by a great fellowship and overshadowed by God. And to this fellowship of those who listen he is to bring a divine awareness, he is to give instruction in religious truth, and he is to communicate a friendliness which encourages, comforts, and helps men to grow.

Such, then, are the great ends of preaching. But what shall we say as to how those ends may be achieved? To make the preacher fit for the fulness of his task is a complex matter. His effectiveness will depend upon what he says and also upon the way he says it. It will be related to his temperament as a man, to his training as a minister, to his technique in the moment when he gives his message. When books on preaching are projected, therefore, they may approach the subject from one of various angles, since no single consideration can well include all those angles of approach at once. There may be books on preaching, as indeed there have been, which center upon the development of the preacher's own religious life. There are others which illuminate preaching through historic study and comparison of some of the great preachers of the ages. There are others which deal with the purposes out of which sermons grow—doctrinal, expository, evangelistic, and so on. There may be books dealing more technically with the minister's methods, with the selection of his themes, the gathering of his materials, the building of his outlines, and the manner of his delivery. Any and all of these have value; but one is more vital than the rest. The man who studies for the ministry will need whatever expert guidance he can get on *how* to preach. But, nevertheless, the more urgent matter both for him and for his listeners is *what* to preach. If there is confusion here, no imaginable brilliancy can make his form of words convincing. And there *is* confusion here, or at least danger of it. Neither those who preach nor those who listen are always quite sure of what the Christian gospel ought to be in relation to the world and time in which we live; but our urgent business is to discover that. No single effort at interpretation can dare to think that it is sufficient; but neither may we dare not try. That is why the title of this book is *The Renewing Gospel*. There is a conception of the gospel, if we can find it and express it, which can make the Christian message come with transfiguring light and transforming power to human souls, and to a whole society, which desperately needs to be made new.

But do men and women in this present time want a gospel? Is this a day of opportunity for a preacher who has an eternal conviction to proclaim? Or will even the fire of a great faith be only like flares plunged into the sea? Is this generation susceptible to a religious awakening, or is this one of the drear periods of disbelief when no spiritual fires will burn? In order to answer that, let us consider briefly some of the tendencies of recent years.

Late in 1919 a deep-hearted and thoughtful servant of his country, Franklin K. Lane, then Secretary of the Interior in the Cabinet of the United States, wrote to a friend who was in Europe: "As for your religion, various of your friends think it odd. I think that you are a subject for real congratulation. A man who can believe anything is miles ahead of the rest of us. . . . John, if you have a religion that can get hold of people, grip them and lift them—for God's sake come over and help us." [1] But what Franklin K. Lane felt was not what most people were feeling at that time. The majority were not crying out for religion. As he wrote to his friend, they would "think it odd"—or else they would not think of it at all. Their minds were filled with other matters. America had won the war, or liked to

[1] *The Letters of Franklin K. Lane,* pp. 324–25.

believe so. The armies were home from overseas. Everybody could get "back to normalcy" and renew the comfortable slogan of "business as usual." We had made a great deal of money during the war. Wages had been high, and dividends higher, and there seemed to be no reason why they should ever come down. We had wheat and cotton and corn, and coal and oil and iron, and factories full of machines to turn out illimitable products, and we faced a world which apparently had to buy what we had to sell. Other nations owed us great debts, and presently they would have to begin to pay. What was there worth having which we did not possess already? As for religion, what exactly might that mean? Citizens who regarded with satisfaction the status of the nation as compared with others liked to proclaim this to be "God's own country"; but what they meant by that phrase was that not only the people but God Himself should properly let well enough alone. When everything seemed so eminently prosperous, why should there be any discontent, human or divine?

In those days therefore there was not much disposition to listen to the preacher or the prophet. One man might call to his friend "If you have a religion, . . . for God's sake come over and help us," but the multitude did not think they needed any help of this description. We were beginning the golden era. If the Harding administration was politically corrupt, it was "practical"; and its sins seemed abundantly atoned for

by the Coolidge prosperity that followed it. Men were
not much interested in God when the convenient gods
of success to which they did homage seemed so abundantly rewarding.

That was one stage in the history of our recent
thought. But another was to follow, and this next was
to be at once more honest and more acid. Men with incisive minds began to show how cheap and thin were the
gilded satisfactions in which the crowd had been content. Sinclair Lewis came with his devastating satires,
and a shame-faced generation began to recognize itself
in Mr. Babbitt, and to see its mean little materialisms
paraded in a Main Street that seemed to run now
through every American town. H. L. Mencken in the
sardonic pages of *The American Mercury* was busy in
the amiable effort of making the average American
citizen familiar with the "Boobus Americanus" under
which classification he was now to come. And Theodore
Dreiser, James Branch Cabell and other remorseless
writers of contemporary literature, were turning their
abilities also to the task of deflating our time's opinion
of itself. They were the representatives of an influence
which in a swift, wide way has been prevailing.

For whatever else our present mood may or may
not be, it is certainly not self-confident. Many false
assurances have been plucked about by the fingers of a
mordant ridicule; and greater and truer assurances also
have been disordered. The self-sufficiency which in the

years immediately following the World War plumed itself like a game-cock has been so stripped of its feathers that it hides in a corner, naked and ridiculous. The cynical forces of this last decade, whether they meant to do good or not, have in some ways surely done it. They have rumpled many smooth hypocrisies. They have blown away many a sham and lie. But the danger is lest they bring another and a different result. They may assail the human spirit with such furious winds of depreciation and contempt that the eyes of all our understanding are filled with dust; and though we may no longer gaze entranced upon little trickeries which masquerade as the truth, we also may be blinded from the sight of truth itself.

Not to see truth, and worst of all to begin to doubt whether any truth exists for us to see, would be the greatest hurt that could befall our time; and of that hurt we have been in danger. A little less than a decade ago, in the most distinguished essay out of many submitted to an American periodical on the subject "What is Youth Thinking?" an able young college instructor wrote:

"Philosophers of decadence reign supreme and scarcely challenged. . . . Everywhere yea-saying is out of fashion, and faith and love are called sentimental, and creative activity is sneered at as futile. Everywhere men make a creed and a faith of doubt, and are sceptics of all but scepticism. The prevailing philosophy is the hard realism of Nero's time—the philosophy of men who rationalize their own impotence. . . . It is the lowest circle of the inferno of our psychological history. We end (like Dante's Lucifer) in ice." [2]

Obviously, the human spirit cannot live in that sort of inferno long. Either it will surrender to it, as a man beaten by a winter storm lies down in the snow to lose himself in numb unconsciousness, or else it will summon up its energies for new and heroic struggle towards its freedom. Clarence Darrow has voiced the mood of those who think that existence is only weary disillusionment which might better drift down into extinction when he wrote in his autobiography: "Emotionally I shall no doubt act as others do to the last moment of my existence. With my last breath I shall probably try to draw another. But intellectually I am satisfied that life is a serious burden, which no thinking humane person would wantonly inflict on some one else." [3] And Theodore Dreiser said: "Life is to me too much of a welter and play of inscrutable forces to permit of any significant comment. . . . I catch no meaning from all I have seen, and pass quite as I came, confused and dismayed." [4] But against that drab hopelessness there is sounding today a more courageous note—as, for example, in such a book as that by a recent university

[2] "What Is Youth Thinking?" by E. Merrill Root in *The World Tomorrow,* January, 1927.
[3] *The Story of My Life,* p. 395.
[4] In a symposium *Living Philosophies. A Series of Intimate Credos,* p. 74.

graduate, William Harlan Hale, which significantly he has entitled, *Challenge to Defeat.* "We have become vividly conscious," he says, "of the bankruptcy of the thought of decadence and dissolution. . . . We are unconsciously, inevitably, desiring a fuller participation of our unified faculties in this spiritual world." [5] He is revolting against what he calls the "overdoing of apartness," or the splitting up of life among sterile theories which keep the whole personality from ever grappling bravely with the realities of life. And if he does not show that he has attained to any very coherent philosophy, to this credo of action at least he does attain:

"We may be the clowns in a comedy for the gods, but we shall play our parts to the finish, and know that our acting is the veriest reality; and when the play is played out, it may not have been so poor a show." [6]

That certainly marks an advance beyond the passive cynicism which had been all too familiar in the years not long past. It does not say of life, as many in effect were saying in the decade before this present one, that

"it is a tale
Told by an idiot, full of sound and fury,
Signifying nothing." [7]

And the will to "play our parts to the finish" makes a long advance beyond that attitude represented by the brilliant but irresolute Henry Adams, as Gamaliel Brad-

[5] *Challenge to Defeat,* by William Harlan Hale.
[6] *Ibid.*   [7] *Macbeth,* Act V, Scene 5.

ford portrays him: "He needed not to think, but to live. But he did not want to live. It was easier to sit back and proclaim life unworthy of Henry Adams than it was to lean forward with the whole soul in a passionate if inadequate effort to make Henry Adams worthy of life." [8]

There is at least a tendency today "to lean forward with the whole soul" toward belief that life does signify something, and perhaps a nobler something—more reminiscent of haunting faiths, more redolent of high ancestral memories—than latterly has been dreamed. Nor has this new awareness been lessened by the economic collapse which our world has had to reckon with. On the contrary, the stripping away of things has made the more thoughtful wonder whether men do not act a better part upon a less cluttered stage. They see that great wealth, when we had it in America, certainly did not guarantee great people. They see that "Man doth not live by bread alone"; and they are not so far as they once were from the confession, "but by every word that proceedeth out of the mouth of God." [9]

So it is that though our contemporaries are not possessed of a gospel, they may be ready to receive one. They are not religious; but the brazen irreligion which has been dinned into their ears is beginning to sound harsh and ugly. They have been disillusioned with many beliefs which their fathers held; but now they

[8] *American Portraits*, p. 56.   [9] St. Matthew 4:4.

are more disillusioned with disillusionment. As T. S.
Eliot has expressed it in *The Rock,* there is——

"A Cry from the North, from the West and from the
    South:
Whence thousands travel daily to the timekept City;
Where My Word is unspoken,
In the land of lobelias and tennis flannels
The rabbit shall burrow and the thorn revisit,
The nettle shall flourish on the gravel court,
And the wind shall say: 'Here were decent godless
    people:
Their only monument the asphalt road
And a thousand lost golf balls.' . . .

"We build in vain unless the Lord build with us.
Can you keep the City that the Lord keeps not with you?
A thousand policemen directing the traffic
Cannot tell you why you come or where you go." [10]

Now it is the business of this book to try to frame a
gospel adapted to the needs of a generation which is
beginning to believe that "we build in vain unless the
Lord build with us." To the "decent godless people"
we must bring a message which shall help them recover
consciousness of that which is divine. We must try to
point to the road whereon men may travel not only to
the "timekept City" but to the "city which hath foundations, whose builder and maker is God." [11]

Therefore this particular chapter is entitled "Some
Blazes on the Theological Trail." That is to say, it is

[10] *The Rock,* by T. S. Eliot, p. 30. By permission of Faber and
Faber, London, and Harcourt, Brace and Co.
[11] Hebrews 11:10.

an attempt to indicate directions in which our thought must go. In such and such a way the effort to formulate the Christian gospel will move if it is to reach a high-road along which men's minds may travel confidently.

• *The first "blaze" to be followed, then, is this:* <u>the Christian message must face facts, and then above these become aware of a greater Fact.</u>

<u>The supreme lesson to be learned from science is its reverence for facts.</u> Science throws here and there the restless searchlight of its hypotheses, but it builds its roads upon the solid ground of facts. If the road cannot be firmly laid in one direction, it abandons that direction and patiently tries another. "Sit down before fact as a little child, be prepared to give up every preconceived notion, . . . or you shall learn nothing," wrote Thomas H. Huxley to Charles Kingsley;[12] and therein he expressed the disciplined teachableness through which the scientific mind has moved on to its triumphs. Religious leaders have not always been so teachable, but they must be if they are to deserve respect. In religion too—indeed, in religion most of all—men ought to be open-eyed and open-minded to all realities. It will not do to have diffused ideas, or mere benevolent purposes. It is necessary that every concrete element of the world that must be dealt with should be taken into account.

[12] *Life and Letters of Thomas H. Huxley,* by Leonard Huxley, Vol. I, p. 233.

There are facts in the realm of religious interest which are sufficiently stubborn. Religion cannot get rid of them; it must somehow incorporate them into the surveyed planning of its own advance. There are all the new facts deduced by modern study of the Bible, in regard to which every preacher must show that he is both intelligent and honest, and furthermore that he is possessed of a spiritual perception which enables him to study the great figures of the Bible in a light which is not less but more significant because of his new knowledge of the sort of men they were and the conditions out of which they grew. There are the new understandings today in the field of comparative religions which enable us to perceive what is unimportant and what is unique in Christianity. There is the fact of the new psychology, and the readjustment which it forces in the conception of human personality and of human consciousness. There is the teaching of the Freudians which has thrown much traditional ethics into confusion. There is an entrenched materialism, both in thought and action, which confronts religion with its belligerent contempt. There is the impatience of the younger generation with orthodox irrelevances. It would seem as though all these things were obvious, but to some they are not obvious. Too many religious spokesmen have never recognized that they are living in the twentieth-century world, and they make great agitation over matters which are no longer crucial. They believe that the way of salvation must lead through their own cult, whether it be through inflexible insistence upon baptism by immersion, or whether it be through a particular interpretation of the mass. They reaffirm their literal interpretation of ancient creeds; they pronounce that "there is no conflict between religion and science," and under cover of that generality they parade old superstitions as though they were admitted fact; and they continue to think that particular insistence upon their own traditions of ecclesiastical organization and procedure touches the vital interests of religion. But meanwhile the urgent interests of most men and women, as they actually exist today, are different. The urgent interests are such as these: the demands of intellectual honesty that religion re-think its formularies in the light of all discovered truth; the need in divided personalities for a spiritual integration; the cry of a disordered world for a redeeming social gospel; the hunger of starved souls for a religion that proves itself not by arguments from yesterday but by demonstration of power today.

There is danger always that men who have been trained in the seclusion of theological seminaries and have breathed, perhaps, an atmosphere which is largely academic may find their thought moving thereafter in a world which is limited, and to that extent unreal. They may be dealing with shadows, shadows cast by history and tradition which are magnificent, but shadows none the less; and they may fail to come to grips with the substance of the real concerns with which most people wrestle. Their need is to see contemporary human beings as they are. They must recognize that the man who desires to be the interpreter of a living faith to this generation takes up a task that will require of him the most rigorous honesty, the most determined mental discipline, and a very steady determination not to substitute smooth phrases for a real analysis of stubborn facts. For it is a fact that there is intellectual confusion which has made people lose sight of all the old religious landmarks. It is a fact that the bewilderments of psychology have made many doubt whether there is such a thing as a soul. It is a fact that social and economic chaos has made many cynical of any spiritual values in our world. And it is a fact that people will have little use for the faith any man holds up unless they see that he has tried to relate it to their own stark needs.

Now, of course, it is always possible that the man in the pulpit, like many other observers of contemporary life, may be overborne by the things he sees. He may add one more to the ranks of the so-called "realists," and his sermons may become a dismal recital of moral and spiritual problems on which he throws no convincing light. He may lead people here and there in tortuous paths of admitted difficulties without ever finding the way ahead toward the hill-top of a great perspective. But his business is to blaze a way through

the jungle of the crowding facts to an awareness of
the Fact which is above all moods and times. That fact
is God.

Of course, the use of that word may seem to beg the
whole question which confronts the Christian gospel
today. Many will declare that a *Fact* is just what God
is not. He is a belief, a wish-fulfilment, a beautiful
but dissolving dream. With this challenge we shall deal
in the fourth chapter. But for the moment we are not
concerned with the full discussion of the truth. We are
concerned with the direction in which the search for
truth is to be pursued. And it is accurate to say that
a great desire in our time is tracing its road by this
mark—the mark of searching blazed by men whose
living experience makes them believe in a divine Reality
which shines ahead.

The messenger of religion must bring with him the
suggestion of Another with whom he has been in touch.
His power to convey that suggestion is not always in
proportion to the wideness of his knowledge of the
lesser facts. It was long ago that the psalmist cried,
"The heavens declare the glory of God; and the firma-
ment showeth his handiwork." [13] We may know a
great deal more about the stars than the psalmist ever
dreamed; but we do not on that account necessarily
surpass him in reverent intuition. In the mass of our
own detailed ideas, the mastery of one great idea may

[13] Psalm 19:1.

escape us. Our own need is to have the nebula of our multitudinous information crystallized round a central truth. The minister of the gospel must be forever drawing the scattered bits of knowledge, which by themselves are only chaos, into the orbit of a larger meaning wherein all things consist. He must communicate the central conviction of God, and this he will do not through words mainly. Rather it will be through something which has evidently happened in his personality. Rudolf Otto, in his great book, *The Idea of the Holy,* has reminded men of the *"Mysterium Tremendum,"* that overwhelming sense of the Divine which fills the soul that once has felt it with a holy awe; and, in the words of another, makes that soul

> "amid all men bear himself thereafter
> Smit with a solemn and a sweet surprise
> Dumb to their scorn and turning on their laughter
> Only the dominance of earnest eyes." [14]

And this obligation of religion through all little facts to bear witness to the Fact transcendent, and the manner of the witness, have been expressed by von Hugel with noble truth.

"We need not try to conceive God: he attends to all that. We have to make room for him in our souls . . . let us rest content. We have not got to invent God, nor to hold him. He holds us. We shall never be

[14] *Saint Paul,* by Frederic W. H. Myers, p. 46.

able to explain God, though we can apprehend him more and more through the spiritual life. I want you to hold very clearly the otherness of God, and the littleness of men." [15]

It is this otherness of God which the great souls have always felt. The message of religion is as agelong as life itself. Always the great Reality is seeking to break through into our human understanding. Always the meaning of God is pressing close upon the minds and hearts of men. It throbs in its immortal rhythm round the coast lines of our spirit, as the tide floods in upon the shore of every continent from the unfathomable fulness of the sea. It shines upon us as the stars shine, with a patience untroubled by the passing of the years. It breathes upon us from the unseen, as winds breathe among the trees.

In the second place, authority for the Christian must be the authority, not of dogmatism, but of discovery.

Dogma in the *Century Dictionary* is thus defined: "A settled opinion; a principle, maxim, or tenet held as being firmly established." So far, so good; but then the definition continues thus: "a principle or doctrine propounded by or received on authority, as opposed to one based on experience or demonstration."

There in those last words is the reason why "dogma" and "dogmatic" have often represented to men some-

[15] *Letters from Baron Friedrich von Hügel to His Niece,* edited by Gwendolen Greene, pp. 17, 20.

thing from which they turned in great aversion. A dogma was a conviction clamped upon them by some external compulsion *not* "based on experience or demonstration." Any reading of history will, of course, reveal that the application of dogma has frequently been as harsh as the definition in the dictionary. Truth has been hardened into formulas, and from these formulas ecclesiastics have built fences within which the minds of men were to be corralled. "Thus saith the Councils," "thus saith the Pope," "thus saith the Church," or "thus saith the Synod," they have proclaimed, "and to their authority the faithful must submit." Often, it is true, men have submitted willingly, believing that the dogma was nothing more nor less than truth itself, expressed more certainly than they alone could possibly express it. But others have rebelled against it, partly because they disbelieved the dogma and partly because they hated to be driven. So it has come about that for great numbers of people, and some of those the intellectually most alert, the word dogma is clothed with repellent associations. It lifts the curtain upon a mental background peopled with sinister figures who could be implacably cruel for what they thought was conscience' sake, and stretching away into shadowy dungeons of the Inquisition and to the glare of lighted fagots where the voices of heretics were smothered in the flames.

Yet it is a curious aspect of the changefulness of our

times that a description such as that just drawn is subject now to challenge. Even as we say that men revolt from dogmatism, we are confronted by evidences which point another way. There is an increasing number who are weary of what they think is the restless and futile wandering of our human thought. They are ready to echo the old words from the Book of Job, "Canst thou by searching find out God?" [16] They are sceptical of the ability of the individual mind or conscience to arrive unaided at any very profound truth. They deliberately turn their faces back in the direction of dogma and to the more dogmatic churches, because in these chaotic and unhappy times they want "a settled opinion" and a tenet "firmly established." They believe that the dogmas of historic faith are the greater because they are not "based on experience or demonstration" if that "experience or demonstration" is an individual matter. They consider that they are based upon a deeper authority, which authority is sought by some in an infallible Bible and by others in the established tradition of an unerring Church. Of such are men like Professor Machen and his Fundamentalist colleagues, founding a new Seminary to safeguard Presbyterian orthodoxy; of such are Gilbert Chesterton and Alfred Noyes in England, espousing Romanism, and T. S. Eliot, changing from his earlier rational non-religion to the philosophy and the cult of the Anglo-Catholics;

[16] Job 11:7.

and of such are those numerous other and less conspicuous persons who sometimes after having long derided any definite religious belief suddenly swing toward one or another highly positive expression of it.

So by a strange reversal of the mood which was prevalent in the latter half of the nineteenth century and the beginning of the twentieth, it is not dogmatism but rather liberalism which is now most heavily assailed. In so far as this corrects an exaggerated swing of thought in one direction and brings the minds of men back to a more sober and thoughtful recognition of the value of the great inherited beliefs, this reassertion of the significance of dogma is wholesome. But those to whom the liberal tradition of a free mind and unfettered inquiry is dear may well take care lest they, in a flutter of timidity, yield unduly to the new reaction. There is danger of exactly this abandonment of the steadier instincts of liberal religion. "Liberalism has pointed us hopelessly astray," men are echoing. "It will never bring men to the goal of an understanding of God. Abandon it, not only now, but always." Young men in the theological seminaries who in their original instincts were liberal, preachers in the pulpits and men and women in the pews, hearing the growing denunciations of liberalism, may be thrown into a panic. They may believe what from many quarters they are told: that liberal thought is bankrupt, and that the only way to save Christianity from drifting into stark negation is to accept what the churches that speak with authority proclaim.

Here then is needed a thoughtful discrimination. The vulnerable point in liberalism is not in its essential nature, but in those exaggerated tendencies with which it is frequently but mistakenly identified. It is assumed that liberalism is humanism, and that these two are the same. Inherently they are not, but too often they are made to seem so. Liberalism magnifies the importance of the individual thinker, and proclaims the freedom of the individual mind. Thus it defends from stifling pressure the human instruments through which truth is to be received. That is a noble thing to do if it is justly done. But the danger is that the balance may not be fully kept. Liberalism may let its concern for the human instruments outweigh its concern for the superhuman truth, in relation to which alone the thinker and his thought have grandeur. It may be so engrossed with man that it forgets God. Then it changes into humanism. It is no longer a sensitive way of weighing truth. It is a biased self-absorption which imagines that the recipient of truth is Truth itself.

Thus liberalism-turned-to-humanism may deserve the revulsion with which many seekers after God react against it. It has talked as though there were nothing in the universe outside its own glib explanations. It has acted as though man creates reality. He can make his own ethics; he can fashion a religion out of his

own instincts; he can evolve a god of his self-engen-
dered ideals. For this sort of humanism the heavens
are empty. There is no Eternal One before whom man
bows down. The sky in which the great stars of the
spirit ought to blaze are fallen, and man walks in an
atmosphere no higher than his own dusty thoughts.

But the true liberalism ought not to be confused
with a humanism of this sort. The liberal spirit is not
insensitive to God. On the contrary, its essential genius
is to be awake to Reality in every sensitive and flexible
way. The religious liberal, whether he call himself
Catholic or Protestant, should know God not less but
more than the man who is only the institutionalist; for
he believes in the vitality and the variety of religious
revelation, and he is expectant of all fresh and creative
ways in which the wonder of God may dawn. In his
thoughts, his hopes and his awarenesses, he is the free
man, because he believes that truth is always free to
lead men beyond the understandings of yesterday into
new disclosures for today. He does not spend his
strength in conserving every jot and tittle of old formularies, as though it were his business "to keep God
orthodox." He, and pre-eminently he—let us be bold
in this time to say it—is the man of faith; for the true
faith is not enslavement to phrases, but courageous
adventure toward the horizons that lie ahead.

Well, then, if the message of religion would avoid
the danger inherent in dogmatism, does this mean that

it must also be indefinite? Must it, perhaps, forego authority altogether? Must it abandon hope of conveying to men a truth which dares to consider itself as sovereign?

No! By all that is most vital, no! For the real authority does not lie in dogmatism. It lies in something which antedates dogmatism, which gives to dogmatism whatever validity it originally possessed, but which in dogmatism is often <u>frozen into forgetfulness, and needs therefore to be warmed again into life.</u> For all dogmatism began with a discovery. Somewhere, sometime, some one pressed through the shell of appearances into Reality. Some illumined spirit, standing on the hilltop of his soul's exaltation, caught a vision of the far horizons which the crowd had never seen. Some prophet proclaimed a truth to which the intuitions of many answered. But how could the truth be passed on to those who originally had not sensed it? Only by clumsy efforts of imperfect explanation. How could the road of the vision be marked for those who had not with their own eyes seen it? Only by sign-posts, by which the swift wonder of the discovery is turned into slow directions. And the nemesis of these second-hand transmissions, the nemesis of the process which turns inevitably into dogmas, is that as time passes men will forget what all the descriptions and directions are for. They will be irked by the precise form of them, and will have forgotten that there is a glory of possible experience to which they are supposed to point. Then the task of a living religion is to wake men to the realization that they can relive the discovery of the great discoverers. They too can enter into an awareness of truth, and the truth thus experienced becomes its own authority.

That is what has happened in the moments of supreme religious experience always. The tradition, which has been like so much dry firewood, suddenly is struck by spiritual lightning into flame. Saul of Tarsus was familiar with what had been the living convictions of the prophets. They had looked for a divine deliverance and a divine Deliverer. To Saul that expectation had become so involved in the dogmatism of the law that he had at first no quick perception of its possible fulfilment. Then on the road to Damascus the discovery came in a flash of understanding. Suddenly he understood the overwhelming significance of Jesus, and saw that "God was in Christ, reconciling the world unto himself." [17] From that time forward he went out into the world with the irresistible authority of the man who speaks, not from hearsay, but from a burning heart. Years went by, and the experience of Saul—who now was Paul the Apostle—crystallized into a dogma in its turn. Paul had to try to set down for others

[17] II Corinthians 5:19.

61

what his discovery had been; and his description of it
became the doctrine of justification by faith. Centuries
afterwards, a monk in the convent at Erfurt wrestled
with this doctrine, finding it at first only an intricate
theology; and then one day, like a man digging in dusty
ground who suddenly uncovers the sources of a gushing
fountain, Martin Luther in one amazed instant of understanding struck upon the living meaning of Paul;
and the joy in Christ which Paul had discovered, redis-
covered now by him, leaped up in his soul like waters
sparkling in the sun. John Wesley in Oxford of the
eighteenth century found again in the same sudden way
the energy in religion which had previously been to him
only an echo. And in our own time, a great mind and
spirit, Albert Schweitzer, could write at first on *The
Quest of the Historical Jesus;* but at the climax of that
book he could proclaim: "He comes to us as one unknown, without a name, as of old by the lakeside he
came to those men who knew him not. He speaks to us
the same words, 'Follow thou me,' and sets us to the
tasks which he has to fulfil for our time. He commands.
And to those who obey him, whether they be wise or
simple, he will reveal himself in the toils, the conflicts,
the sufferings, which they shall pass through in his fellowship, and, as an ineffable mystery, they shall learn in
their own experience who he is." [18]

[18] P. 30.

That sort of revelation of living truth seems a far cry from dogma. And yet, as we have already suggested, there is no ultimate contradiction between true experience and dogma truly understood. For the new experience of the living person may be only his rediscovery of what some immemorial dogma long ago has proclaimed, and that which the individual thinks he has discovered ought always to be purified and expanded by the longer verdict of the ages which the real dogma is simply an effort to describe. It was not a representative of any authoritarian religious group, but a Congregational minister who wrote these discerning words: "The prophet disintegrates old standards; the priest must integrate new ones; and that is a very hard thing to do. It is disastrous to life to be all the while in a prophetic whirlwind. . . . The priest is not therefore to be too seriously blamed for becoming a dogmatist. This is the function we have assigned him. He must integrate and construct, collect and sort and arrange his materials, and build a habitable house of truth. He can, of course, do much more than priests ever have done to prevent the tyranny of old dogmas. He can say at the end of every list of standards or ideals: Moreover, it is one of the tenets of our system to be always expecting change and always working for progress; it is one of the articles of our faith to make earnest with the doctrine of the continued revelations of the divine Spirit. This, too, is a dogma, but one that turns the flank of the dilemma of prophet and priest." [19]

A third mark of any message which seeks acceptance in this time ought to be that it is conceived not so much in terms of finality as of fertility.

It may seem that the trend of the times runs otherwise. There are influences in the world which do arrogantly claim finality. They insist that they have exclusive truth; they propose to speak the last word. Hitler announces in Germany that the Nazi movement "will last a thousand years." Mussolini announces that liberalism is dead, and that the Fascist will henceforth be the master. The Soviet Republic is equally convinced that the philosophy of Karl Marx and the program of Lenin will presently silence every contradiction. It is a dangerous conviction—dangerous in each case not only for the tranquillity of the world, but for the particular force which boasts of its infallibility. For when any body of opinion believes that the last word has been spoken it starts upon a cruel dogmatism which some day will cause the human spirit to rebel against it. Anything which calls itself final outrages the variety which life ultimately insists upon for its own expression. It is not by its claim to finality, but by its ability to make a social order fertile for its full possibilities, that any social theory will at last be judged.

[19] *Art and Religion,* by Von Ogden Vogt, p. 85 f. Yale University Press.

The same truth holds in the realm of religion, though often and stubbornly this may be forgotten and denied. It is finality, and that alone, which many religious teachings have been most bent upon possessing and upon being acknowledged to possess. Religions have claimed finality for their dogmas and for their discoveries too. Not only in teaching but in life it has been assumed that the traditional pattern must be duplicated in order for the whole religious experience to be accounted valid.

But as a matter of fact, the vital religious experience never merely rediscovers what the discoverers of another generation have proclaimed. Paul does not mechanically reflect his Master; his soul was athrill with the fact of salvation through the love of God, which he had caught from Christ, but he had to express it in his own way and in his own words because only so could he make his message living. Martin Luther entered into new worlds of spiritual understanding through gateways which Paul had opened for him, but he explored then other pathways than those in which Paul had exactly walked. And Christian believers today may find again with sudden joy the wondering release of the gospel of justification by faith; but they will not wait to put it now in Luther's words. The gift of the creative souls is not to fasten others within the limits of their creation but to wake creativeness in them. The great explorers of the world of spirit give to those who follow not so much their maps as their imagination, not so much a specification concerning where they went as enough of the joy of their going to make these others also want to go.

Even in relation to Jesus himself—as in the fourth chapter we shall more extensively consider—it is not "finality" that a vital gospel wants to stress. It is true, of course, that in great ways he was and is final. If we know anything at all about life's redeeming forces, we know that love is ultimate; and the love which he expressed from Bethlehem to Calvary cannot be transcended. But "final" and "finality" are stifling words. The danger in them, and the actual tendency in their use in Christian doctrine, has been to build a fence round understanding. Orthodoxy has often borne itself as though its duty was to define what has been rather than to proclaim what might be. It has been so narrowly concerned to recognize nothing but what Christ authorized that it has been blind to the widening implications of Christianity. It has been jealous of anything that seemed to go beyond Christ, and as a result it has often blocked the way to those beyond-nesses of thought and life into which the living spirit of Christ himself could have been the guide.

Thus we have the sort of conscientious intolerance which admits nothing that is not believed to have been established by those canons of authority which are considered final. Take, for example, the matter of church government and ministerial "order." Nearly all Christians express a desire for Church Unity. But Roman

Catholics and Anglo-Catholics and Eastern Orthodox
and high-church Presbyterians, each group in its particular way, conceive that there is a certain form of the
ministry which was ordained by Christ himself; and
some consider that to compromise their own form would
be to betray the finality of what Christ directed. So
with the early creeds, and the decisions of the great
Church Councils. These also are final, says the inflexible defender of tradition; they are "the faith which was
once delivered to the saints." [20] But this once-for-all-
ness may prevent their recasting into terms of contemporary thought by which the faith may be again set
free.

Or take the still broader matter of the relation of
religion to every-day life. At innumerable times Christian people have resisted the application of the Christian
gospel to practical affairs because they said they could
find no warrant for this relationship in the New Testament, which was final. It is quite true, as they have insisted, that the New Testament contains no specific guidance as to how the Christian spirit is to deal with the
cruelties of modern industry, or with economic privilege
and economic servitude, or with civic corruption, or
with war. But this obvious fact becomes paralyzing only
when the idea of "finality" has brought men's imagination to a standstill. Then what they call "the pure gospel" becomes only a past gospel, with no present and expansive power.

[20] Jude 3.

What is needed is the different word and the different idea. It is the *fertility* of the gospel which supremely matters. It is not that something was revealed once to be finished; it is that something was revealed which is never finished. In God's meaning as made plain in Christ there is an influence which goes on fertilizing wide areas of life of which the first century could not have dreamed. To argue too much about finality may wither religion at its root; to be joyously concerned for its illimitable fertility and to take care that its spirit shall energize every creative purpose of the centuries, is to make it "final" in the supreme sense that it will be expressed in every one of life's triumphant ends.

Once again, a gospel which would be satisfying must illuminate both the near and the far.

Out of his own experience, Doctor Richard C. Cabot wrote once a memorable essay entitled *Foregrounds and Backgrounds in Work for the Sick.* He outlined the two aspects of the imaginative physician's opportunity: his chance in the first place to see, and to respond to, the hesitant hopes and fears of the human individual who is his patient, and by the human touch of kindness in the little things to help that person to feel secure; and in the second place, his chance and his duty to move through his ministry to the individual into a larger understanding and a larger mastery of those

causes of sickness with which preventive medicine ought
to deal. But the words he used have a wider reference.
It is not only in the work of the physician or in ministry
to the sick that "foregrounds and backgrounds" need to
be regarded. All religion must be related to these. Any
gospel for men's full life must take account both of the
crowding facts and of the far perspective.

It must touch the human spirit with friendly intimacy
in its obvious human needs. It must show that it understands what people are doing and what they are wanting
every day. It must give to men and women help in their
homely responsibilities and show them that there is a
kind of heroism which can be expressed in what look
like unheroic things. It is not the people who are in-
cessantly talking about or listening to large programs
who may be producing the values which keep society
sound. Queen Victoria used to be much irritated by
Mr. Gladstone when he was Prime Minister because, she
said, "he talks to me as if I were a public meeting"; and
people who need personal help in religious matters too
often are put off with being talked to as though they
were a public meeting, and public opinion too. It is
well—as we shall remember presently—that every humblest individual's consciousness of himself and of his
daily duty should be set against the background of
destinies larger than his own; but nevertheless he must
see the simple foreground first. The business of the
Christian gospel, and the business of the Christian

preacher, is to recognize with sympathy and to interpret with imagination what the individual man and woman actually is feeling. It is not enough to have earnest ideas on the subject of unemployment; it is necessary to have a message of strength and courage for the one who is unemployed. It is not enough to have a generous vision of a new society; it is necessary to have a word of inner discipline for the prosperous man and of encouragement for the poor man who has got to fit into society now. No matter what beneficent changes may be wrought hereafter in the social framework, life could never be anything but mean if the individuals in society were mutually hateful, or even if they were cynical, blasé, and bored. In the foreground of every true picture of the things worth desiring must be set the simple virtues which people one by one must be encouraged to achieve: the sense of responsibility, faithfulness to what they undertake, the sort of honor which carries a job through with unfailing workmanship when no one else is watching, considerateness for others, and the everyday goodness which shows itself in "the little unremembered acts of kindness and of love."

So much for life's foregrounds. But one emphasis, however important it may be, must not obscure the wholeness of the truth. Men need a consciousness of the backgrounds also. They cannot long be content to be haphazard atoms fitting into no great plan. What is it all for? they ask. They ask that about their work; they ask it about life itself, and about the whole matter of its standards and its aims. The best men are not satisfied simply because they happen themselves to have food and shelter and enough to live on. They wonder about the world their children will inherit. They look at the stupid injustices which lay such unequal burdens on other men. They want to feel that what they do is contributing to something better which will develop. Among many contradictory opinions as to this or that aspect of the social revolution in Russia, this seems to be an almost unanimous recognition: namely, that the people of Russia are inspired by a great hope. They are willing to endure cruel hardships now because they believe that a golden day of happiness and plenty waits for them, and that they are going straight ahead to reach it. So a Christian interpretation of our social order and a Christian purpose for it must be able—and more nobly —to create the background of a great belief, if a Christian message for this age is to be prevailing.

But there is a still loftier background to the full picture of life which religion can lift up, and one without which at long last the human spirit must find itself unsatisfied. It is the background of the answer to those questions which are ultimate. Even if all life were comfortably adjusted in material affairs, and even if we had achieved the far objectives of social justice, and even if all people were living together in moral decency, still there would be a restlessness in the human soul. Still there would be the old echo, "What is it all for?" For unless there be a spiritual Reality in the universe, and unless these human strivings of ours have some validity in a purpose which is infinite, then what is all our human turbulence but a little whirling of the dust upon the surface of a presently-to-be-extinguished star?

To lift us from that mood, with its continual possibilities of disintegration and defeat, we need the consciousness that life's real values are measured, not by our time, but by eternity. We need again the message of the transcendent God. Many non-religious men can hold fast to their duty with a stoic courage; but it is the religious man who can invest his own faithfulness with a sort of radiance which makes his spirit like a bright torch from which other men can rekindle their dying flame of courage. On the fiftieth anniversary of his ordination to the priesthood, at a time of rejoicing after the long tragedy of the World War, Cardinal Mercier said this: "Whether in the years of peace or the years of war, whether in poverty or prosperity, whether in failure or in success, never have I failed to feel deep down in my heart, a sense of tranquillity, confidence and peace. . . . I must tell you the secret of Christian serenity. It lies in giving yourself confidently to the goodness of the Lord." [21]

Upon that note, we are led to the summing up of all

[21] *The Life of Cardinal Mercier,* by John A. Gade, p. 254.

that has been said concerning the gospel which is needed now. Through all and above all it must be exactly that —a gospel. That is to say, it must be the message of good news. There is already enough sadness and bewilderment in the world. Men do not want to listen to a spokesman for religion and come away saying what Robert Louis Stevenson said in the pages of his journal: "Went to Church today, and was not greatly depressed." They want the flaming message of a conviction which gladdens and inspires. It is this sort of a gospel which Christian people must show forth as with "the power of an endless life." It should be a gospel which takes account of all crowding facts, yet is most sure of one great Fact; which rests its authority not on dogmatism, but upon discovery; which is concerned not with finality, but with fertility; which interprets the near and friendly foregrounds, but also the august and awful backgrounds which make up the grandeur of human life; and makes its proclamation through the lips of those who cry, "Woe is unto me if I preach not the gospel[22]—for the love of Christ constraineth us." [23]

[22] I Corinthians 9:16.   [23] II Corinthians 5:14.

73

CHAPTER III

THE JESUS THAT WAS AND THAT IS

THE former chapter concluded upon the theme
with which this one must begin. "The love of
Christ constraineth us." [1] That has always been
the authorization of the Christian preacher, and the dynamic of the Christian gospel. It must be so still. If
Christianity has something unique to give the world, it is
primarily not a philosophy, nor even a program. It is
the living figure of one by whom all its thinking and its
planning are inspired. It is Christ. In years before and
in years since, the Christian message is still the same as
that which Samuel Rutherford voiced three centuries
ago: "O come all and drink at this living well; . . . no
man cometh and is not welcome, no man cometh and
rueth his voyage; all men speak well of Christ, who have
been at Him; men and angels who know Him well say
more than I now do, and think more of Him than they
can say." [2]

Yet even though it be true, in Rutherford's quaint
words that "all men speak well of Christ who have been

[1] II Corinthians 5:14.
[2] *The Loveliness of Christ; from the Letters of Samuel Rutherford*, p. 67.

74

at Him," it must be recognized that not all men are of this sort. Many have not been "at Him." To many he is only a name, distant, unreal, it may be irritating. There are writers who have tried to prove that he never lived. Others think that though he did live it would have been better for the world if he never had. They consider that the principles he proclaimed are thin vagaries, incapable of dealing with the rough realities of this world. He seems to them a dreamer and a sentimentalist, and they regard him with a mingling of patronage and of pity because of that. Or else they think of him as the responsible cause for the Christian Church, which they dislike. He seems to them the root of intolerable dogmas, of harsh ecclesiasticisms, and of stubborn prejudices which hold the minds of men in bondage.

It is plain, therefore, that Christ himself is the key position in any discussion concerning the Christian gospel. If he stands, the whole line stands. If he should fall, it would be like the falling of Verdun. Nothing else would be capable of saying to the forces of non-Christian doubt and denial: "They shall not pass."

Let us consider then what Christ is and what he means, and how his meaning must be presented if our world is increasingly to acknowledge his significance.

In the first place, of course, there is the question raised by writers such as Arthur Drews[3] and P. L.

---

[3] *Die Religion als Selbstbewusstsein Gottes* (Strasbourg, 1925).

Couchoud[4] as to whether the Jesus of the New Testament ever did exist. It is a question which must be recognized, at least. But it is not one which needs to be dealt with at serious length. The weight of affirmative evidence, and the affirmative judgment of great scholars and thinkers, are so overwhelming that the denial of the few is left to seem little more than fantastic special pleading. The letters of Paul, the first of which were written within twenty years of the crucifixion, the story of the rise of the Christian Church as recited in the Book of Acts, and the graphic narrative of the first-century synoptic gospels, furnish such a wealth of almost contemporary description as exists in connection with very few of the unquestioned figures of ancient history. Any book which alleges to disprove the actuality of Jesus will be, of course, a seven days' wonder; but authoritative historical scholarship has weighed that matter and come to its clear conclusion. And the common sense of men at large perceives the fact as clearly as the specialists, and with perhaps even a quicker instinct. Ordinary folk who are accustomed to judging truth simply, and not by tortuous argument, know that when there are great effects in this real world there must be some cause great enough to have produced them. They know that much does not flow from nothing. And when they see that through century after century of history there has flowed an influence peculiarly personal, taking

[4] "L'Enigme de Jésus; Le Mystère de Jésus," in the *Mercure de France,* March 1, 1923, and March 1, 1924.

multitudes of the strongest men and women of every generation and making them witnesses to a spirit which they say is the spirit of Jesus Christ, they recognize that these things could not be unless there had existed the tremendous force of personality which was Jesus himself. When men taste the salt far up an inland river, they know that water from the ocean has brought it there. When they see the flooding of the tide, they will pay scant attention to those who tell them there is no such thing as the sea.

There is another phase of contemporary thinking which must also be recognized in any effort to understand Jesus. An important group of New Testament scholars, though dismissing as idle the once exploited theory that Jesus never lived, have stressed the exceeding difficulty of reconstructing any positive outline of his life. This *form-geschichtliche Schule,* so-called in the German word that is not effectively translatable, points out that the materials in the Gospels are not put together as an objective historical narrative, but are rather schematic—being impressions of Jesus' figure and of his teaching as these had taken shape in the faith of the early Church. So, as one of these critics writes, "The figure of Jesus is not directly accessible to history . . . not what he was, but what he is, is all that is revealed to the believer." [5]

This school of criticism, like every other one, is apt

[5] *The Life of Jesus,* by Maurice Goguel, translated by Olive Lyon, p. 59.

to ride hard in the direction of a newly perceived idea. It may lead opinion off into a by-way that is not the central road of balanced truth. But even if the contention of this school were more fully allowed than now it is, the central fact stands no less commanding. For that fact is this:—that whether or not we can reconstruct an adequate biography of Jesus, the strangely self-evidencing quality of his spirit shines through the records which we do have. As Goguel has voiced the truth in his new *Life of Jesus,* it is not necessary to press "the demand for history to give a certitude which it cannot give, for a certainty which actually adheres only to religious intuition and to faith." [6] The personality of Jesus has transcended the imperfect documents. It is a fact which generations of Christian experience have attested that a definite and unique character makes himself known to those who try to let their spirits be attuned to his.

Passing then beyond these preliminary questions concerning the attestation of Jesus, the prime business of the Christian interpreter is not to argue about him, but to describe him. The reason why men ever do doubt his existence is because they have not, in Rutherford's incisive phrase, "been at Him." When his figure emerges fully from the printed page, and when he is really seen, then the vitality and the vividness of him carry their own conviction. We do not want to begin with theological conclusions. That is to reverse the natural process. We

[6] *Ibid.,* p. 60.

do not want to begin with the Christ of the creed-makers, nor with the remotely throned Christ of the stained-glass windows and of the formal sculptures in the reredos behind the altar where worship is offered in his name. There is truth in the impulsive words of one of the most discerning modern writers on the life of Jesus: "The more I see and feel him, the more it seems to me it was friendship he came burning to give (and to receive) ; and it was a cold requital that instead we gave him worship." [7] And many will echo what Canon Charles E. Raven has written in *A Wanderer's Way*, as he described the confusion between the formalism of religious instruction in an English boys' school and the awakening religious hunger of his soul for a companionship such as that of Christ. "He is so plainly the hero that I wanted, the hero who was not merely strong but sensitive and sympathetic, brave and yet tragic, lonely and wholly lovable. If only He had been as real as Cæsar; if only I had known His story as I knew the Iliad; if only my teachers had not put a halo on His head, and talked affectedly, or not at all, about Him; if they had treated Him as what He is, the greatest and most alive of the Sons of Men; then the passion pent up within me would have found its object; my affection and my mind would have been His; I should have been given the friend that I was seeking." [8]

[7] Winifred Kirkland, author of *Portrait of a Carpenter*, etc., in a personal letter.
[8] P. 29.

What we need then is that preachers, and others who may try to be interpreters of the meaning of Jesus, should help us to see him as the first disciples saw him, when the Man above all others walked among living men. We want to see him in his human vividness; in his tenderness and in his strength; in his gaiety and in his gallantry; in his tremendous hours of joy as well as in his hours of tragedy. We want to frame in our minds a picture of him as he went along the shores of the Lake of Galilee, where the fishing boats were lying, and by the magic of his word made men want to leave those boats and start on an adventure of which they knew nothing except that they were going to be with him; or the picture of him watching the children playing in the market-place, and taking them up in his arms; or the picture of him in the house of Simon the Pharisee, when the woman of the streets knelt weeping at his feet and rose up forgiven and redeemed; or the different picture of him as he strode in terrible indignation through the courts of the temple, and before the irresistible authority of his face the traders and hucksters who had defiled it trampled upon one another's heels to get away; or the last majestic picture of him as he stood silent and unafraid before the judgment seat of Pilate and went through the streets of Jerusalem to Calvary, saying to the women who lamented along the roadway, "Weep not for *me*."

The recurrent fact of history has been that, in all the

Christian centuries from the earliest ones down to our own time, when men have thus thought of Jesus, a unique thing has happened. He has become no longer a figure in the past. The thought of him is not bare abstract knowledge of some one who was once and is not now. Suddenly the knowledge comes alive into experience. He draws men's minds and hearts again to him. He possesses them as immediately as once he possessed the disciples. He becomes the interpreter of all the values of this world. To live as he lived is seen to be the highest destiny of our manhood. To believe in God as he believed, is to have the clue to the meaning of our universe. As long as Jesus exists, then the whole of reality has beauty and purpose and hope. Innumerable men and women have felt what Sir Wilfred Grenfell has put into words when he said, "Amidst just such shifting scenes the highest reward of life to me would be to be like Jesus." [9]

Yet words like those last must be read in their profounder meaning. "To be like Jesus" may express an ideal as spacious as infinity; but on the other hand, it may suggest a self-assurance which is only shallow. The saying so much heard a decade ago, that "what we want is the religion *of* Jesus, and not the religion *about* Jesus," wears thin. We cannot get the religion of Jesus so easily as some have been fain to think. Out of our own resources to believe as he believed, dare as he dared,

[9] *What Life Means to Me,* p. 30.

and attain the character which was his, is not within the scope of our contrivances unless these human energies of ours are baptized by a diviner flame. It will not do to say smoothly: "Jesus was good, and so let us be good. Jesus believed in the fatherhood of God and the brotherhood of Man, and we shall be like Jesus if we take that same motto." It is necessary that we go on to understand a vaster truth *about* Jesus; and that is the fact which gave to the first disciples a sense of awe in the midst of their devotion, namely, that in him, something tremendous had come into the circle of human existence from the Otherness of God.

It is here that we must see the widening significance of the distinction suggested in the preceding chapter, between the facts and the Fact. It is possible to know a great many facts about Jesus and yet never to understand his significance. Even the most diligent New Testament scholars have sometimes shown the likelihood of that. A man may spend his life studying the questions involved in the stories of Jesus' birth, or the problem of the relationship between the Synoptic Gospels and "the Gospel of John," or the apocalyptic element in Jesus' teaching and its connection with contemporary hopes. He may lavish on these or other intricate matters great patience and zeal for truth; but when he is all through he may know little or nothing of the secret of Jesus' place in the history of human souls. He may have acquired all the facts; but the Fact rises above the level where his scrutinizing eyes have peered. In a recent book about Japan, by one who lives there, is this description of a woman traveller from the west who on her first visit to the Orient stood on the deck of the steamship as it entered Tokyo Bay:

"Her eyes eagerly searched the scene before her, from the shore line to the green hills along the horizon. Finally she exclaimed, with a note of disappointment, 'I cannot see it!'

" 'What are you looking for, Madam?' asked one of the ship's officers standing near.

" 'Oh, I wanted so to see Mount Fuji,' answered the lady.

"Instantly came the answer 'Look higher!' " [10]

And as the visitor did so, there before her lifted eyes the shapely cone of the peerless mountain, snow-capped and gleaming, rose far above the clouds.

It is the instinct of the lifted eyes which gives to so-called orthodox Christian theology—and Christology— the immemorial strength which it does retain. Much liberal thinking is meticulously true, but true on a dead level. It sees realities which are horizontal; it does not so readily see those which are lifted high. Traditional theology is often clumsy in its expression and heavy with prose when it is attempting to describe awarenesses

[10] *Typhoon Days in Japan,* by Robert S. Spencer, p. 153.

which can only be conveyed in poetry; but it is right in its stubborn insistence that what it has seen is more than any humanistic phrases can express.

But teaching about Jesus and belief about Jesus must always be re-vitalized by the second of those considerations which in the preceding chapter were seen as blazes on the theological trail, namely, the recollection that dogma is nothing unless it continually represents a discovery. Even the most elaborate of the Christologies have their roots in a discovery. They may have gathered to themselves other elements which have not grown from that central root, as a tree may be overgrown and sometimes almost strangled by vines that climb upon it, or fed upon by parasites that sap its strength. The task of clear thinking is to distinguish the tree itself from its encumbrances, and to know the ground from which it springs.

Consider in this light some of the great beliefs about Jesus.

The supreme one of these, of course, is the doctrine that Christ was more than the highest upreach of humanity toward God. He was the entrance of very God into human life. This is the shining central faith of the Incarnation.

Now it is plain, of course, to any one who reads Christian history that this doctrine has often become a barrier of separation rather than a bond of unity. It has been built into a rigid fence of definition which divides by difference of creedal words those on the one hand deemed to be Christians and those on the other who are denied to be such. It is possible for the doctrine of the Incarnation to be preached in our own time so that the winsome beauty of it is lost and it becomes a sterile thing of words. If one would see how true this is, let him turn to such a book as *Gandhi of India,* his own story as edited by C. F. Andrews, and read there of the way in which, when Gandhi was a young man in South Africa, over-zealous but not over-intelligent Christians presented the meaning of the Incarnation to him.

Always the need is for interpreters in the pulpit and understanding disciples in the pews who see the doctrine of the Incarnation in terms of a discovery. The first disciples made a discovery before they made a doctrine. They found the power of God coming to them through Jesus. They felt it long before they could phrase it, and we today must likewise remember that what makes a man a Christian is not the phrases he assents to but the feeling toward Christ and in Christ by which his soul is seized.

Look back to the beginning, and see how the experience and then the expression grew. Those who knew Jesus and followed him from Galilee, and all those who like Paul were mastered by his spirit, were possessed with the immediate consciousness of a transfiguring spiritual power that flowed through him. They expressed it in the terms which sprang most spontaneously to their thought. "Who do men say that I am?" asked Jesus one day of his disciples, and then, turning to the twelve, "Who say ye that I am?" [11] And Peter cried out his instant, unpremeditated answer, "Thou art the Christ!" It was the most that he could say to express what overwhelmingly he felt. Jesus was Messiah, the tremendous Deliverer who summed up in himself all his people's agelong hope for the fulfilment of God's promise. Paul the Apostle wrote to the Romans that "the gift of God is eternal life through Jesus Christ our Lord": [12] and then, in words that broke into music like a song, he wrote of those who were "more than conquerors through him that loved us," [13] and of the assurance that neither "height, nor depth, nor any other creature, shall be able to separate us from the love of God, which is in Jesus Christ our Lord." [14] The writer of the Epistle to the Hebrews wrote of Christ as being the brightness of God's glory and the express image of his person. And the fourth evangelist in the prologue of his Gospel identifies Jesus with the *Logos,* which is God's eternal message of his meaning to mankind; and he writes that "In the beginning was the Word, and the Word was with God, and the Word was God." [15]

All this was discovery breaking forth into the fervor

[11] Mark 8:29.   [12] Romans 6:23.   [13] Romans 8:37.
[14] Romans 8:39.   [15] John 1:1.

of speech. In every case the one who speaks uses the metaphor which seems most complete and real to him. What he is trying to do is not to fasten upon those who might listen a form of words. He is trying to transmit a spiritual experience.

That is what also the later and more formulated Christian theology was endeavoring to do. It was constrained to express what it knew was inexpressible, since it understood, with the great Apostle, "the depth of the riches both of the wisdom and knowledge of God," [16] and like him might cry out at the moments of its best awareness, "How unsearchable are his judgments, and his ways past finding out!" [17] But a tendency grew, as it always does when the first flush of discovery begins to fade, to become more engrossed in the formal expression than in the vital spark of the thing expressed. Theologians began to suppose that if they were learned enough, and diligent enough (and unhappily, as it sometimes appeared, if they fought one another furiously enough in church councils) that they could find philosophical terms which would adequately set forth exactly what Jesus was. Consequently we have the Nicene Creed, the Chalcedonian Formula, and other elaborate efforts to fathom and measure the personality of Jesus according to the specifications which Greek philosophy and the other though-forms of the fourth-century and the fifth-century world, astronomical, psychological,

[16] Romans 11:33. [17] Hebrews 9:3.

and metaphysical, might furnish. It was set forth with an orthodox precision which was to silence all question that Jesus should be held as "Very God of very God; Begotten, not made; Being of one substance with the Father." And the Athanasian Creed was to add to these and other promulgations of orthodoxy the warning: "which faith except every one do keep whole and undefiled, without doubt he shall perish everlastingly." [18]

It is beyond question that the creeds have had imperishable value in the history of Christian thought. They reveal the ways in which men tried to account for the immensity they felt in Jesus. They stand as a continual challenge against any glib and hasty modern thought which reckons that it has accounted for him by forgetting that his meaning is immense. But the danger of the creedal and conciliar dogmas is that ultimately they may put the test of Christian discipleship on an untrue basis. They exaggerate the form of words above the living faith.

A general fact is best made plain through a particular instance, and one particular instance may have an importance far beyond its immediate issue when, like a vane, it shows the way the wind is blowing. In the winter of 1934, after the Dean of the Cathedral of the Church of England in Liverpool had invited two eminent Unitarians to preach in the Cathedral on special occasions, a protest against this action was lodged with

[18] *The Book of Common Prayer of the Church of England.*

the ecclesiastical authority. The fact that men who belonged to a Christian fellowship which does not affirm the orthodox creeds should thus preach in a Cathedral of the Church of England was considered as "a scandal in the face of Christendom." There was no protest against what either of these ministers had said. Both of them were recognized to be men of devotion, both in their characters and in their utterance. Nevertheless the House of Bishops of the Convocation in the Province of York declared itself to be of the opinion that an invitation to preach, even at special services in the Cathedral, should not be extended "to any person who does not hold, or who belongs to a denomination who does not hold, the common Christian faith in Christ as 'Very God of very God'; 'Who for us men and for our salvation came down from heaven,' 'And was made man.' "

Consider now what it means to make those words in their literal rigidity the test of Christian recognition. They carry upon the face of them the reflection of the thought world of sixteen centuries ago. They were framed by men who conceived the universe according to the Ptolemaic astronomy, and who, when they wished to express the coming of the divine into human life, thought of it instinctively as the descent of the Son of God from a heaven which was almost within range of vision above this earth. They were thinking of reality not primarily in terms of living spirit, but in terms of Greek metaphysics, which made them use the concep-

tion of substance as being the basis of Jesus' oneness
with his Father. Interpreted in its historic perspective
and considered as a symbol of the truth, the creed of
Nicæa has revealing value; but to make its words today
a substitute for flexible and imaginative recognition of
the living Spirit of Jesus is to show how possible it is
for men through their dogmas to cease to be discoverers.
What is it that shows men to be Christians? Three brief
sentences in the Fourth Gospel suggest the sufficient answer. "We would see Jesus":[19] there is the essential
desire. "He that hath seen me hath seen the Father":[20]
there is the illumination. "He that hath my command-
ments and keepeth them, he it is that loveth me: . . .
and I will love him, and will manifest myself to him":[21]
there is the sign and seal of loyalty and acceptance. The
only vital Christian unity must be bound together by
some such living tie of spirit as those words represent.
It is not that the phrases of the Nicene Creed are untrue.
It is rather that when they are made a rigid measure-
ment of men's faith they are too inelastic and too stiff
with ancient terms of thought to register sensitively
what the faith of present people really is. To hold that
none have entered into the fulness of Christian discipleship unless Christ means as much to them as he meant
to those who wrote the Nicene Creed is one thing, and
a right thing. To say that no one loves Christ completely,
and exalts him as Lord, unless he expresses, or belongs

[19] St. John 12:21. [20] St. John 14:9. [21] St. John 14:21.

to a communion which expresses, Christian loyalty in the same words which the men of Nicæa used, is another thing and a very unhappy and mistaken one.

Of course there are those who will shrink back frightened from such a representation as this. They are busy with their formal attempts at what they call Christian reunion. They hold world conferences on faith and order, and debate among themselves how the various historic communions may be brought together. They are greatly afraid, and not unnaturally so, lest any one communion should abandon what others consider orthodox, and therefore make a mutual approach the more difficult. But the insignificant result of conferences of this kind already held ought to make evident this truth, that any effective and united Christian witness for the years ahead will not be reached by timorously looking backward. It will not be reached by insisting that all men alike shall put their convictions into the more ancient phrases. This sort of engrossment betrays a fundamental fear. There is among many ecclesiastics, and especially among some of those who are chosen to go as representatives to meet ecclesiastics of another name, the tendency to regard religious inheritance legalistically. "The faith once delivered" [22] is conceived as like a title-deed. However old it grows, and however faded may be its ink, it must be kept sacrosanct, for the heritage of faith depends upon it. Change one letter, and

[22] Jude 3.

no matter how much Christianity men may seem to have, technically they must be assumed not to have it because their right to its inheritance is no longer valid. When reasoning proceeds in this manner, it is quite understandable and inevitable that if a person has an unorthodox name, such for example as Unitarian, no matter how Christ-filled as an individual he may be, he is, nevertheless, not a Christian. And another person, though he may be spiritually obscurantist and intolerant, nevertheless is a Christian if his ecclesiastical title-deeds are secure.

This sort of insistence that Christian faith must be identified with a form of dogma is blindness to the urgent realities of life. Suppose when the British Expeditionary Force crossed the Channel in 1914 the military authorities of France had said, "We cannot believe in your community of purpose unless you use our language. We do not want you as allies unless hereafter you will speak French." Obviously it would have been more convenient if they did speak French. It would have made adjustment easier; but nobody ever considered the idea of making a common cause depend on that condition. And why not? Because the desperate necessity of a common danger brushed all secondary matters out of the way. The tragedy is that Christians often do not realize that they too face the sort of desperate need which can make men of different ecclesiastical language into blood brothers when they see it and face it together.

The world today is dark with the forces of paganism and international savagery. It is mobilizing in many nations those spiritual denials which challenge the reality of Christ. What we need is a Christian solidarity not of men who are agreed in a form of dogma but who are agreed in the passion of their great discovery—men who for themselves have found the power of God in Jesus and recognize their brethren in all others who reflect that same Incarnate Lord.

Pass on now to another of the formulated doctrines about Jesus. Here again the great opportunity of the preacher is to interpret the faith of the Church in such wise that what is secondary shall be distinguished from what is essential, and that always men are led back to repeat the discovery, not of language, but of life itself, rising new and beautiful in Jesus.

For many centuries there has been a doctrine of the Virgin Birth which, in the words of the *Catholic Encyclopædia,* teaches that "the Blessed Mother of Jesus Christ was a virgin before, during, and after the conception and birth of her Divine Son";[23] and this doctrine "was defined under anathema in the third canon of the Lateran Council held in the time of Pope Martin I, A.D. 649." [24] The emphasis which the Roman Catholics place upon this doctrine is repeated also by the Fundamentalists among Protestant communions. "The lib-

[23] *Catholic Encyclopædia,* Vol. 15, p. 448.   [24] *Ibid.*

eral preacher insists on the possibility of believing in Christ no matter which view be adopted as to the manner of his entrance into the world," writes Professor J. Gresham Machen; and he goes on to say, "But such an impression is radically false." [25] Many Christian men and women have been taught to hold the conviction upon which Professor Machen here insists, and they believe that their trust in the unique value of Jesus depends upon their believing that he was born, not of Mary and Joseph, but of Mary alone by miraculous conception, which separates the manner of his birth from that of all others whom our human race has known.

It would be, of course, a limitless task to attempt to trace the history and effects of this dogma. That in its developed aspects, overgrown though it be with Mariolatry and other strange excrescences, it has been a comfort to innumerable people goes without saying. But the vital matter is to attempt to understand its origin. And here it may be boldly said that it began with something simpler, more vital, and essentially more beautiful than itself. The original discovery of the disciples about Jesus was not concerned with considerations of a Virgin Birth. What they discovered was that in him a strangely new and potent influence had come into their world. They felt this long before any one began to talk of a Virgin Birth as the reason and the explanation of it. The earliest Gospel, that of Mark, has no slightest hint

[25] *Christianity and Liberalism,* by J. Gresham Machen, p. 108.

of such a doctrine. Neither do the letters of Paul the Apostle, who certainly did not depend upon any such teaching as this to validate his supreme conviction that "to know the love of Christ, which passeth knowledge" is to be "filled with all the fulness of God." [26] Neither does the Book of Acts, with its accounts of the teaching by which the first Christian converts were won, make even so much as a suggestion of a Virgin Birth. Whatever else may or may not be true, therefore, this indubitably *is* true, namely, that the earliest and greatest interpreters of Jesus, proclaiming his Saviorhood in ways that certainly seemed to them sufficient, included in this sufficiency no concern for the manner in which physically he was born. They knew in their own experience the grace and power that came through Jesus. At first that fact stood by itself without elaboration; but presently in the Christian community there woke the instinctive impulse to glorify this fact and also to explain it. It was evident that Jesus had communicated something greater than ordinary experience knew. How then should the greatness of Jesus be adequately expressed? There were traditions among the world's religions of saviors who had been virgin-born. Then why not Jesus? Once the question had been asked, or once within the Christian fellowship the wondering suggestion had started and had begun to spread, belief in it sprang up instinctively like a flame. Among the Chris-

[26] Ephesians 3:19.

tians of that age, uncritical and naïve, their thought of
what thus appropriately might have been became the
conviction of what was. Like many other unspoiled
people, they were poets, and it is the poetry of worship
which is singing in the lovely stories of the Virgin in
the introductions to the Gospels of Matthew and of
Luke.

Of course, there are those who will say that this is a
misleading and inadequate description. The doctrine of
the Virgin Birth, they maintain, was based upon a direct
communication of the facts from Mary herself and
therefore is history. But to say the least, it is obvious
that this can never now be proven, and it is further true
that our developed thought of the uniqueness of Jesus
does not depend upon the explanation which the early
Church thought appropriate and convincing. As poetry,
the story of the Virgin Birth has imperishable loveliness, because it was the symbol, true and natural to
that age, of that matchless significance of the Child
of Mary which all succeeding ages equally have known.
But that which was the·spontaneous form by which faith
explained itself then is not spontaneous now. Recognition of the incomparable spiritual power of Jesus does
not in this period of Christian development make itself
dependent upon assurance that he was miraculously
born. It is curious to see how this abandonment of
primary emphasis upon the doctrine of the Virgin Birth
is revealed in the utterances even of those conservative

spokesmen whose desire is to maintain it. A small gathering of the bishops of the Protestant Episcopal Church, meeting in Dallas, Texas, in November, 1923, in an environment and under influences which made liberal thinking difficult, put forth a statement reasserting the Virgin Birth with vehemence, but then went on to say: "It is not the fact of the Virgin Birth that makes us believe in our Lord God, but our belief in Him as God makes reasonable and natural our acceptance of the fact of the Virgin Birth." [27] That is to say, in relation to the faith here asserted the Virgin Birth appears not as cause, but only as a corollary.

The truth is that the traditional doctrine is at best only an "over-belief" to the original and continuing belief-that-matters. This central belief rests not upon the proof of anything secondary and derivative. It rests now, as it did in the beginning, upon discovery. It is the inner knowledge of what Jesus is, because of what he does today. He is known to be God's supreme Son because of the way in which he does communicate the life of God to multitudes who through him are awakened to their sonship.

It would be wrong to think that such an interpretation as we have outlined makes Jesus any less divine than he has been made by the terms of what might be called a

---

[27] *Pastoral Letter of the House of Bishops of the Protestant Episcopal Church, Issued from a Special Meeting in Dallas, Texas,* November 15, 1923.

more orthodox tradition. Rather it makes his divinity more vivid and understandable. For we conceive of the divine reality now not in static terms. We conceive it in the living terms of consciousness and will. God's essence is not in some metaphysical substance to be conveyed through miracle, but in that which His Spirit is and does. God's nature is the perfect expression of holiness and of love. He desires that man, His creation, should be righteous and loving. But man, being finite and sinful, is neither one except very dimly. If, however, there is produced a human soul in which righteousness and love are made perfect, then that soul has achieved God's ideal destiny for humanity, and at the same time has been completely God in human life. And it is this that Jesus was.

Though the terms have changed greatly, the meaning here of a completed Incarnation is the meaning which Athanasius was contending for when he rightly insisted that Jesus was *homo-ousios* instead of *homoi-ousios*. That is to say, in Jesus we see, so far as human existence can reveal it, not an approximation only to the meaning of God, but the very certainty of God Himself. Or to put it in another way, there is nothing in the infinity of God which is inconsistent with what we find in Jesus.

It is sometimes asked: "Can we say that our Lord Jesus Christ as God was begotten before all worlds, and as man was created?" To which the answer must be this:—The Christ-ness that was in Jesus and that made him Christ is eternally begotten; or, put in other words, the infinite God of holiness and love whom we know through Jesus, has forever been willing and purposing such an expression of Himself as came to pass historically in Jesus. That was the eternal *Logos,* the forthgoing Word of God. In the Incarnation this *Logos* first found its complete utterance through an actual human life. Thus, though Jesus had complete humanity in all the accidents of time and circumstance, he had a divinity which was begotten before all worlds. And the fragmentary divineness in every human soul is that soul's response to the *Logos* which only in Christ was made complete.

As with the birth of Jesus so with the death. There have been expressions of doctrine which must be led back into experience if they are to be convincing. Upon no other aspect, perhaps, of Christian faith, has so much been thought and written as upon the doctrine of the Atonement. Here, the learned have said, is the heart of the Christian gospel; and though the unlearned often could not understand, somehow they have felt that this is true.

It would, of course, be an impossible task to try to set forth here even an outline of all the theories of the Atonement. Many of them are obviously outmoded now. Some of them in the perspective of later years seem very crude; but the important matter is to recapture those tremendous convictions which every doctrine of the Atonement has somehow tried to express.

The first of these is the <u>sense of human sin</u>. That has not been foremost in our time. We were almost ready to believe that man could smoothly accomplish his own salvation; but the little shallows of a generation's brief complacency are swept from sight when the deep tides of the inexorable returning truth roll in. Whatever we imagined a score of years ago, we are ready to admit today that human folly and sin are very real and very tragic. As William Temple, the Archbishop of York, has said: "If any one feels that the language which the Church asks him to use is exaggerated—'We do earnestly repent, And are heartily sorry for these our misdoings; The remembrance of them is grievous unto us; The burden of them is intolerable'—then let him think of slums, and sweating, and prostitution, and war, and ask if the remembrance of these is not grievous and if the burden of them is not intolerable. Let him remember that these horrible things are there, not because some men are outrageously wicked, but because millions of men are as good as we are, and no better." [28]

Multitudes in the world will recognize facts like those and admit them to be regrettable; but it is the Christian who will see that they are sins, and who furthermore will see that in the corporate sense of that word he himself is

[28] *Federal Council Bulletin,* June, 1933. By permission of His Grace, the Archbishop of York, England.

involved. This will be true of him exactly in the measure
in which he has contemplated the cross of Christ, for sin
then will seem to him no impersonal matter. It will be
part of that moral tragedy which crucified once, and
which crucifies again, the Spirit of Jesus, and the potential evil in his own heart will seem to him more terrible because he perceives it to be exactly the same sort
of evil which produced the crucifixion.

Some of the great doctrines of the Atonement made
much of the thought of ransom. Christ by his death
bought the redemption of mankind from the sin and
condemnation in which it was held. The particular forms
of those theories are to most modern thought impossible.
We cannot follow the ancient thinkers who said that
Christ's death was a ransom paid to the devil to whom
mankind has been delivered through Adam's fall.
Neither can our thought accept the doctrine of other
theologians who said that Christ's death was a ransom
paid to the justice of God the Father which must thus
be satisfied before his love could be free to forgive. But
what we do need to rediscover, and indeed are rediscov-
ering in this our time, is that somehow and somewhere
there is a terrible barrier to men's salvation which can
only be broken down at an awful cost. No one can look
at human life today and not see that it is in bondage; in
bondage to ignorance, in bondage to malevolence, in
bondage to strange perversions of the best in man, for
which the old superstition of the devil's acquired do-

minion was a crude but graphic symbol. Human nature will not be redeemed today by any easy process. It
must witness again the love of God crucified on its behalf. Christians who have pondered the meaning of the
cross will recognize the fact of it as repeated in every
idealist who suffers contradiction, in all great leaders
who are willing to be martyrs for the sake of truth, in
all those Christlike souls who for the sake of justice
within the social order, or for peace between the nations
may be willing, as Christ was, to face both the rulers
and the mob and to go to their own Calvaries. They
will understand the truth which George Bernard Shaw
expressed in the epilogue to his *Saint Joan:*

"*De Stogumber.* I did not know what cruelty was like.
I had not seen it, you know. That is the great thing: you
must see it. And then you are redeemed and saved.

"*Cauchon.* Were not the sufferings of our Lord Christ
enough for you?

"*De Stogumber.* No. Oh no: not at all. I had seen them
in pictures, and read of them in books, and been greatly
moved by them, as I thought. But it was no use: it was not
our Lord that redeemed me, but a young woman whom I
saw actually burnt to death. It was dreadful: oh, most
dreadful. But it saved me. I have been a different man ever
since, though a little astray in my wits sometimes.

"*Cauchon.* Must then a Christ perish in torment in every
age to save those that have no imagination?" [29]

But the rediscovery of the meaning of the Atonement
is the rediscovery of something more than sin and of

[29] P. 154. By permission of Bernard Shaw.

the cost of redemption from it. It is the rediscovery of that invincible love of God which was expressed in Jesus' willingness to die. One of the great saints and spiritual seers of our generation was Geoffrey Studdert Kennedy, and no man agonized more than he did over the awful fact of sin and suffering. As one of his friends wrote of him after his death: "To him the supreme consolation was found in the thought that God also suffers. The Cross was for him no incident of our Lord's human experience only: it was the center of the Gospel Revelation of God." [30] Then, however, that same interpreter goes on to say: "But if this is really all that can be said, then for one who realizes the burden of evil as he did, suicide is the only reasonable course—or would be if we could only be sure that it procured annihilation. What makes the thought of suffering in God a comfort and inspiration is the fact that the very Name of God stands for Power and Joy, so that to think of suffering as something real in Him is to think of the reality of suffering as swallowed up in the joyous victory of love triumphant through sacrifice." [31]

If in our day men in the Christian pulpit will preach again the Atonement in that fashion, then the agelong dogma will become again the discovery of the way by which life may be redeemed. And always, of course, it may be remembered that it is not from the pulpit only that the meaning of the Atonement is proclaimed. At

[30] *G. A. Studdert Kennedy. By His Friends,* p. 220.
[31] *Ibid.,* pp. 220 f.

the heart of all Christian worship is the everlasting sacrament of the Communion. Through that sacrament Christ, not in theological formularies, but in living fact, can be to us an atoning Saviour. He can make us see our own sins and our wretched, cowardly surrenders as part of that same evil by which the love of God is here and now newly crucified. He makes us understand that there is no failure of ours, however callous we may be, which does not issue in a cross for some other soul that loves us, and which, like God, is sensitive to the disloyalties we try to cover and forget. And this same Jesus of whom the sacrament of the broken bread and the poured-out wine reminds us, this Jesus unafraid to die, and forever dying until he can lift us also into life, is at once the most tender and the most implacable fact in all this universe. He will not let us go. He will not let us rest until we have stopped crucifying the grace of God and are ready instead to crucify the littleness within ourselves, that from *that* crucifixion we may rise to the fulness of life which he would have us win.

The distinction between discovery and dogma appears again in reference to the resurrection.

On Calvary the disciples watched the physical death of Jesus. They thought that he was dead and all their hopes dead in him. The kingdom and the glory that were to come through him had vanished like a broken dream.

But presently the amazement of a new fact dawned. They became aware again of Jesus. They said that they had seen him—seen him in the garden, where his body had been laid in Joseph of Arimathea's tomb after the crucifixion; seen him on the road to Emmaus; seen him in the Upper Room. The accounts of these experiences are written in the Gospels, but not with cool and calculating precision, as scribes would write. The flame of a mystic emotion quivers in them, and their details can no more be reduced to one precise and finished pattern than the lights of an aurora can be caught in one stiff sketch. Here and there the colors overlap; here and there they cancel one another; but the whole effect is as of a never-to-be-forgotten glory springing from some unearthly source. The accounts of the resurrection will not give us a consistent answer to many questions which might be asked concerning the manner of it; what they do give is the picture of men and women lifted out of despair into radiant confidence through their sudden certainty that the Master whom they had loved was again alive. Nor did they only *think* that. They went out to *live* in the strength of it, to dare death in the joy of it, and to build in the light of it a spiritual fellowship which has gone on growing from their day to this.

When the resurrection is conceived thus as a discovery, vital souls in every generation can enter again into its experience. But when literalists desiccate it into their particularized dogmas, then the quickening wonder of it escapes. Ecclesiastical assemblies and stubborn creed-makers are always provoking that tragic loss. They think they must lay down hard specifications as to what the resurrection was and how it happened, and exactly what the nature of the appearances to the disciples must be conceived to have been. But when they hammer together their wooden definitions they are like men who think they will protect a skylark, when all they do is to stifle its song and see it die, once it is imprisoned behind their heavy bars. There is nothing that so effectively and so surely will kill belief in the resurrection as dull insistence upon the way in which it must be believed. Truth-loving minds are offended, and inquiring minds are balked, when they are told, for example, that it is necessary to believe in the reanimation of the physical body of Jesus which was crucified in order to believe in his resurrection. Thus the whole reality becomes entangled in intellectual contradictions, and the possibility of a spiritual awareness is lost. The one thing of importance is that contemporary men and women should be made to understand that they can enter into what was the heart of the experience of the first disciples. They do not have to submit to a dogma; they can repeat a discovery. They can learn that the personality of Jesus is not dead and buried in a distant time—but that it can come as living power to enlighten the mind, to sensitize the conscience, and to inspire the will of those who look for him today. And this can be equally true whether or not they may be given those mystic experiences of sight and sound which have come to some great souls in every generation, so that they have said—like the disciples of the first century—"I have *seen* Christ." It is not seeing that is at the heart of certainty. "Blessed are they that have not seen, and yet have believed." [32]

"I envy not the twelve,
    Nearer to me is He;
The life He once lived here on earth
    He lives again in me." [33]

It is true also that even that doctrine which often seems most intricate and baffling, the doctrine of the Trinity, can be resolved again into the original experience out of which it grew, and from which experience repeated a clearer understanding can grow now.

In the Book of Common Prayer there is a collect for Trinity Sunday which voices this petition "Almighty and everlasting God, who hast given unto us thy servants grace, by the confession of a true faith, to acknowledge the glory of the eternal Trinity, and in the power of the Divine Majesty to worship the Unity; We beseech thee that thou wouldest keep us stedfast in this faith." It is safe to say that for most persons that petition will seem little more than a clat-

[32] John 20:29.
[33] *Thoughts for Every-Day Living,* by Maltbie D. Babcock, p. 173.

ter of abstruse words, and if they gain from it any thought of the Trinity it will be of something far too recondite for ordinary mortals to concern themselves about. But the lack is in the words and not in the reality. The reality which the Christian Church has tried to reflect in its doctrine of the Trinity is something very vital and inspiring.

For this is what essentially it embodies:

Once there were certain persons who were destined, it seemed, for nothing more than humdrum life in the little towns of Palestine. They had in themselves the same mingling of good and evil and the not-yet-good which all human nature has within it. Mostly their lives moved on very ordinary levels, bounded by the uninspired calculations, the little selfishnesses and the small contentments which make up a physical existence. But they knew that this was not all. If mostly they walked in the dust, they also had glimpses of the sky. Always there was something winged in their souls, little fluttering aspirations toward greater heights of courage, faithfulness, and devotion. Usually they did not ponder much about this double aspect of their natures, but they knew it was there. They knew that often something within them, which yet did not seem to originate within themselves but to come from elsewhere, made them catch glimpses of a far-off beauty, and made them want to be better than they were.

Then into the ken of these men and women came

Jesus of Nazareth. They followed him because he was so magnetic that they could not help it. They loved him as men love a beautiful compelling friend. Then they began to see that in Jesus there was made real before their eyes the fulfilment of all that spiritual grandeur which they had glimpsed through little intimations in themselves. He gathered up in his character and made complete the broken ideals which they had thought of. He made them understand what it was that in their best moments they had wanted, and he showed them their dim conception of an altogether abundant life lifted up into luminous fact. And as they lived with him and thought about him, and as they entered more intimately into companionship with him, their thoughts took a wider range. He made them think of God. He made them have a feeling of God's reality which they had never had before. The sort of life he led before their eyes always was suggesting the coming in of a power from beyond the borders of this world. When they looked at Jesus, they said to themselves: "This is the way life must be when it is not human only but divine."

But there was a question which they had to answer, a question that did not arise when things were bright but did become insistent when the dark days came. Jesus was what all men ought to want to be: they were sure of that. Jesus was what a good God would want to give to the world as His best gift: they were convinced of that. But was God as good as Jesus, and was a God like Jesus "Lord of heaven and earth," as Jesus had believed? This was what the first disciples, on days such as that of the crucifixion, wondered, whether or not they ever put it into words. And this is the question which Christian thinkers in later years have had to repeat and for which they have had to seek an answer.

The doctrine of the Trinity is the attempt to formulate the answers which men have drawn forth from their experience and from their hope. It is the expression in words of the conviction which life was shaping. What the doctrine of the Trinity essentially says is this: that the three great aspects of fact and of faith are all true, and all rest in the reality of God. The little winged things in men which lift them above their common selves are not mere accidents of chance emotion. They are God the Holy Spirit. The love of Jesus is not simply one lonely upthrust of human endeavor. It is the revelation of the divine meaning which from the beginning of time has been trying to incarnate itself in human fact. And the invisible God, the reality upon whom our whole existence rests, is actually the One whom Jesus called his Father. Here was the basis upon which the theologians built their dogmas, for what the theologians have been trying to do was to anchor in the nature of God Himself those experiences which men wanted to be sure were validated.

Sometimes the philosophy of the doctrine has obscured the religion of it; but the religion at its heart is after all a relatively simple thing. It is the faith that those glimpses of divineness which men feel within themselves, and that perfection of life which they have seen in Jesus, and the almighty love and power upon which through all changes and contradictions they can depend are all one, and are all God.

We pass on now to another main division in our thinking. Let us set the thought of Christ in the third of the distinctions suggested in the preceding chapter. Religious authority ought to be based, not on finality, but on fertility.

The obsession of theologians often is that they must get something finished. They want to work out a definition that does not need to be redrawn. They are avid to attain a once-for-all-ness, both of religious fact and of religious phraseology. Therefore they are busily seeking to discover precisely what the earliest Church believed, and said, and did; and if they can trace those elements in its thought and life which are assumed to be directly traceable to the words of Christ, then these are final. So, for example, they delve into the question of the sacraments. So also they try to find (with many different answers) what was the original form of the organization of the Christian Church, and what were the orders of its ministry. And when any particular ecclesiastical group has settled upon its own answer to these questions, then it concludes that the particular principle which it has read back into the first century must be authoritative and unchanged forever.

But this way of thinking leads straight into a serious embarrassment. For when religious teachers continually stress the fact that the Christian gospel as found in the New Testament is final, they lay themselves open to the disturbing questions of the practical world as to why Christ said nothing about matters with which our modern life is of necessity concerned. "We go to the Gospels," men say, "and we find there is no direct light on many of our most insistent problems. The Gospels do not tell us how to put religion into our modern industry and business. They say nothing about politics and how to keep these from being pagan. Jesus lived in a world utterly different from our own. He has given no counsel directly applicable to men who live in the machine age and must somehow adjust their consciences to an economic and social complex such as first-century Galileans never dreamed of. If you insist on calling Jesus final, then the conclusion is that religion is inapplicable to the kind of world in which we live."

But the real truth which ought to be proclaimed grows out of a different word. <u>It is the fertility of Jesus which makes him timeless.</u> He did not deal directly with many of the questions which beset us now. He could not have done so in that civilization of Palestine and have been intelligible. But his "final" authority, in the sense that his enlightening Spirit reaches through to the ultimate ends of our considering, lies in those seed suggestions which bear their characteristic flower in every sort of situation. Doctor Henry Sloane Coffin has quoted the revealing remark made to him by a high Chinese official, not a Christian, who said that, having studied the various religions of the world, he concluded that they were much alike in many of their aspects, but that he was ready to acknowledge this difference in Christianity: that it has through Christ "the power to create a more delicate conscience." [34] Moreover, the particular Christian conscience has a quality which is unmistakable. Though they cannot put it into words, even simple folk know what it means to endeavor to be "Christlike." The life which Jesus lived and the values which he made evident do create an ideal which makes men instinctively know when they ought to be discontent with any situation, and what, at least, is the general nature of change they ought to aim at if the facts as they exist are to be set right. And it is in connection with this fruitfulness of Jesus rather than in any creedal definitions that have to do with finality, that the test as to whether any particular life is Christian or not is rightly made. What counts is not that a man should repeat phrases about Jesus which are supposed to be final; what counts is rather that those who see him blossom

[34] *In a Day of Social Rebuilding*, p. 15.

into characteristics which are Christlike should say of him instinctively, "He has the root of the matter in him."

And so we come to the fourth, and for this chapter the concluding, aspect of the significance of Jesus. In him both the foreground and the background of life stood revealed.

Through the life of Jesus the bare and simple facts of our everyday existence have received a dignity which no other influence has ever given them. The little things which lie in the forefront of our life, the everyday thoughts and emotions which are common to every human personality, have been shown to possess an inherent greatness which no accidents of worldly fortune are needed to enhance.

Consider the lovely story of the beginning of the life of Jesus. What is it that we listen to? It is the story of a man and woman coming at the end of a weary road to a little town on a darkened hill, knocking in vain for shelter at the door of the village khan, a forlorn harborage in a stable, and there in the dark of the winter night, when the whole of the indifferent world outside slept uncaring, the birth of Mary's child. In such simplicity the gospel of redemption is begun. It is as though the Spirit of the meaning of the universe had said: "I will not let you think that in some rare place and privilege life can attain its infinite fulfilment. Here in a lowly place, here in the commonest environment, I come to dwell with you. Here, and not elsewhere, is Emmanuel."

When Mary's child was born there in the stable on a winter's night, with no warmth to give her comfort except the warmth that came from the bodies of asses and of oxen lying near, the vast indifference of the Roman world, unknowing and unconcerned, seemed to smother that event in Bethlehem with all the weight of its remote contempt. What did it matter to Cæsar that a peasant mother in one of the far-off provinces held a baby in her arms that night? What contemptuous laughter would have rung from the lips of Roman legionaries if it had been suggested that there in the child's life was a power more enduring and more irresistible than their swords. To the calculations of the world the fact of the child Jesus would have seemed a thing utterly devoid of consequence.

It was true that this child of Mary had no accidents of this world to make him great. He never had any wealth. He never had any exalted social or official rank. He had no powerful alliance among the forces of his time. He grew up in a little town of the hills of Galilee among the peasant people of a lightly regarded province, and moved on through his short career to end upon a cross. Yet the personality of Jesus so transfigured those facts of his existence that he remains today as the one great influence from those ancient years which reaches across the centuries with an immortal power. Cæsar Augustus and all the glory of his empire are gone, and the long-vanished centuries are the winding-sheet in which the dead glories of Rome have descended into the dust. Herod is only an ugly memory, saved from being utterly forgotten because his name is associated with Jesus, whom as a child he is said to have sought to kill. But in the living personality of Jesus innumerable people, through all these nineteen hundred years, have found the incentive for a larger life.

"I need wealth to make me great," men often think. "I need some pedestal of privilege and importance to lift me high. Give me great and shining material, and I will build a shining career. Give me a long start in the race of life, and I will go far." That is what we are often tempted to think and to desire; but the message of God is different. Out of the little things, the simple things, all greatness can be wrought.

"What looms so dark, my goodman, across the whitening
    moor?
A little door, my master, naught but a little door.
A little door so low, a little door so spare!
O wondrous thing that Christ the King
Should deign to enter there." [35]

Moreover, as it was in the midst of simplicities that the life of Jesus began, so it was with simple people and in simple places that most of his work was done. If

[35] *The Little Door,* by Van Tassel Sutphen.

his life entered this world through a little door, so also
it was through little doors that as a man he went in and
out. His friends were of the fishing-fleet of Capernaum.
The homes he knew were in the little houses of ordinary
folk there in the fishing-town, or such an undistin-
guished home as that of Mary and Martha in Bethany.
He dealt with people in their ordinary occupations, and
his parables were drawn from his observation of the
work of every day: from the woman kneading bread,
the sower casting seed into the furrow, the shepherd
guarding his flock, the worker in the vineyard pruning
his vines and watching the ripening of the grapes.
Much of what he did with people was to make them
feel how worth-while *their* work could be and to give
them a new inspiration for what they had to do. Some
of his great acts of healing seem to have their secret in
the fact that he could communicate to men and women
a new will to live because in his presence life became a
more joyous thing. It was this, perhaps, which happened that day when he went into Peter's house at
Capernaum and Peter's wife's mother lay sick of a
fever. When Jesus went into the room where she was
and laid his hand upon her, she not only felt the fever
leave her, but, as the Gospel of Mark goes on to say,
she rose up and "ministered unto them." [36] Even the old
routine of the household work was suddenly made
beautiful now that Jesus was there. And so likewise he

[36] Mark 1:31.

117

opened the eyes of people everywhere, including the eyes
of his own disciples, to see a new and divine significance
in things they had counted common, as in the lilies of
the Galilean field, in the nesting birds, in the play of
little children in the market place.

It is not too much to say that wherever the life of
Jesus is known the perspective of this world's values has
been altered. Men may not live up to the truth they
know; but they know the truth that it is not the conspicuous things which are the great things, but that
greatness lies in those least material facts through which
a noble purpose shines. Jesus said once to his disciples
that among the Gentiles those who exercised authority
—and by that he meant those who exercised authority
for their own ends and for their own benefit—are called
benefactors; "but so shall it not be among you." [37] The
prophecy of his words has come true. In civilizations
which have the Christian ideal as an instinct by which
to judge, the benefactors are recognized to be those who
live in simplicity and in self-forgetfulness in order that
they may serve a higher loyalty. A man like Thomas
Mott Osborne who goes himself to prison in order that
he may understand the prisoners' lot, women like Jane
Addams and Lillian Wald who take upon themselves the
burden of the unprivileged and the poor, the teacher,
the scientist—all these are bearers of the torch which
the love of Jesus lighted. It was with a true instinct

[37] Mark 10:43.

that Henri Labouchère, referring to the rude little laboratory in Paris where Pierre and Marie Curie followed the long search that led to the discovery of radium, called it "a scientific Bethlehem."

But the significance of Jesus would not be fully understood if thought should stop with his effect in magnifying the inconspicuous and the common things. He threw a new light upon all this foreground of everyday affairs; but also he built against it always the background of infinity. He made men remember God.

It is an error therefore to represent Jesus as essentially a teacher of ethics. Many modern commentators have been prone to that mistake. They want to rationalize their conception of him, and to separate this from the profounder aspects of religion in which they do not feel at home. It seems to them an embarrassment that Jesus should be considered to have had beliefs which introduce the supernatural. They prefer to think of him as a kindly teacher of the Golden Rule, a preacher of the high morals of the Sermon on the Mount, the imaginative observer of the actual world who could draw from his observations the practical interpretations which he put into his parables. And others, approaching him from another angle of particular desires, find in him the sort of prophet which *they* want. They regard him as the first of the social revolutionaries, the friend of the poor man and the enemy of the rich, whose Kingdom was to be a new order of social justice which men by their own determination were to build. In either case the figure of Jesus moves upon the plain of purely human forces. There are no cloud-capped mountain peaks of the majestic loftiness of God on which also his spirit is to be recognized as at home.

But the fact is that Jesus is not Jesus without recognition of that atmosphere of the supernatural which constantly he breathed.

Now, it is true unhappily that the word "supernatural" has been so used as to become almost repellent to many modern minds. It has been so associated with obscurantism, and with the tendency of many ecclesiastics to multiply dogmatic assertions about the unknowable as an alibi for refusing to deal squarely with the known, that "supernatural" and "irrational" have come to be thought of as interchangeable terms. There *is* thus an unworthy teaching of the supernatural, a crude and uncritical assertion of the miraculous, and a use of cloudy phrases by pompous ecclesiastics whose zeal is greater than their effort after knowledge. But the essence of belief in the supernatural, as William Adams Brown has pointed out in his recent notable book, *God at Work,* is belief that above this material universe and in all our human life there is the power of One who is *spiritual, creative,* and *perfecting;* and that miracles are all those great experiences of a life larger than our own which bring us *wonder, enlightenment, fortification, and fulfilment.*

In *this* atmosphere of the spiritual and the miraculous Jesus lived and moved. Never did he lend encouragement to the idea that human life can be recreated out of its own resources. He was not other-worldly in the sense of dwelling abstractedly in a realm of consciousness remote from ours, but he was other-worldly in the sense that he felt the power of another world impinging constantly on this one. Human life to him was like an estuary opening to the ocean and feeling forever the mighty rhythm of the tides that set in from the sea. He believed that whatever was worth accomplishing on this earth must be accomplished by God Himself, and that man's part is not to invent, but to listen, to understand, and to obey. "My Father is greater than I," [38] he said. "Why callest thou me good? there is none good but one, that is, God." [39] Thus in his vivid hyperbole he expressed the truth that the utmost which the human spirit can reveal will be beautiful only in proportion as it reflects that which already exists in God. He looked to God for his own strength. He drew from long vigils of prayer the illumination of his purpose. Students of the Gospels have not yet been able to answer surely what the apocalyptic conviction of Jesus was—and doubtless never will. It is impossible to say with precision how he felt himself to be Messiah, and what he believed he was destined to achieve; nor to say fully what he thought as he went up to Jerusalem to be cruci-

[38] John 14:28.   [39] Mark 10:18.

fied, and why he chose to die, and what he expected to
happen in and through his dying. But one thing is unmistakable. He believed himself to be in the hands of
an eternal power and an eternal love. He lifted up his
eyes to the mountains, and found there his sufficient
help. Overshadowing all the foreground of every day's
contingencies was the background of his certainty of
God.

CHAPTER IV

CAN WE TRUST THE GOD OF JESUS?

IT is not sufficient to gain a wide agreement among thoughtful people as to the nobility of Jesus. Most of those who have regarded him at all will say that he represents the high peak of human possibilities. In strength, in purity, in tenderness, his character had a rounded beauty and a moral grandeur which make him tower like a great mountain above the lesser heights of men. If our general conception of the meaning of human life could take its direction and perspective from the level of Jesus, then the right progress of mankind would be more nearly assured.

To say that this would be unanimously acknowledged would be, of course, to go beyond the facts. There are those who will not admit desirable excellence in Jesus. Some—like Nietzsche—deliberately regret and repudiate the significance of his life. They want a world shaped by principles which are the antithesis of his— ruthless where his were compassionate, self-aggrandizing where his were self-forgetting. And there are others who admire the beauty they find in Jesus, but with sadness. They wonder whether what he believed and the way he lived can ever be considered "practical." His ideals seem at times to them like <u>lovely castles built only of dissolving clouds.</u>

Nevertheless, when all is said, it remains true that his manhood exercises in the main a compelling fascination. Multitudes who admit that they cannot wholly understand him, and are sharply conscious that they follow only haltingly in his way, realize that they cannot get away from him.

> "Still with unhurrying chase,
>   And unperturbed pace,"

an inescapable something in Jesus, like the *Hound of Heaven,* pursues them, and in their own acknowledgment they cannot turn aside from the track which he compels.

But it is at another and further point that difficulty begins. Many will say that they can acknowledge the greatness of Jesus the man; but they cannot believe that he was "the son of God." His humanity is commanding; but to talk of his "deity" seems to them to introduce ideas from which they revolt.

And this revolt may spring from one or the other of two quite different reasons. There are some who do not like to think of Jesus in terms of God because, as the result of crude and clumsy teachings which sometime they absorbed, God seems to them distinctly unattractive. They would rather think of Jesus only as a beautiful

human figure desirably kept separate from the sub-
conscious feelings which the word "God" rouses in them
—feelings which may trace back to unpleasant child-
hood moments when they heard somebody read the
story of Elisha, who, being a good man, could get God
to send bears out of the wood to eat up teasing children;
or when they looked at the old-fashioned wall mottoes,
"Thou God seest me," and thought they would be much
more comfortable if He would look the other way.

And on the other hand, there are others who are disturbed when they try to conceive the relationship between Jesus and God not because this suggests anything
disagreeable, but because it suggests a bewilderment
which is almost despairing. Not a great while ago,
multitudes of people who said they could not believe
that Jesus was divine would at the same time say with
emphasis, "Of course I believe in God." This belief of
theirs in God had never been very clearly considered;
they were not sure exactly what it meant, but they did
have an implicit assumption that there must exist a
great Cause and Creator. They thought of God as a
mighty Being, real though inscrutable, majestically busy
somehow keeping the universe in order. They could not
understand very well how this sort of God could be in
the Jesus who walked in Galilee. The two ideas of a
God on the throne of power and God in a man among
men were hard to reconcile. Nevertheless, they assumed
that a God who is altogether powerful and altogether

good did manifest Himself in Jesus. But now, even among men who want to be religious, there grows a troubled wonder. There is a moral doubt as to whether any God at all exists. A *moral* doubt, be it noted and not an immoral one, as some controversialists who call themselves Christian like to imply. A moral sensitiveness to the seeming tragedy of life, a recognition of inescapable evil in the universe, a haunting doubt as to whether there is any power of goodness dominant over the blind drift of matter and the cruelties of chance— these things make some men begin to think that all conception of a God outside ourselves has got to be abandoned; and that if Jesus is to be called divine, it is because of what men's reverence for his character has made him, and not because of what he was made by any something or some one from above.

To the first group, those whose idea of God is so crude that the whole association of the word is disagreeable, we may well bring the striking words of Professor Whitehead in his *Adventures of Ideas*. He wrote: "The progress of religion is defined by the denunciation of gods. The keynote of idolatry is contentment with the prevalent gods. . . . In all stages of civilization, the popular gods represent the more primitive brutalities of the tribal life." [1]

"The denunciation of gods . . . !" That sounds at the first echo like a description of atheism, rather than

[1] *Adventures in Ideas*, by Alfred North Whitehead, p. 125.

a description of religion. Nevertheless, Professor Whitehead is right. The progress of religion is measured by the denunciation of those gods of men's distorted ideas of what divinity is, in order that the real divineness may shine through. The whole Bible, to say nothing of other religious literature, reveals that fact. Religious progress has been the gradual ascent of the consciousness of men from the valleys of their ignorance to those heights of clearer awareness from which the grander perceptions of God came into view. "The popular gods" did "represent the more primitive brutalities of human life." The Israelites were constantly being led off into the pagan worship of the Baalim, or of Ashtoreth, or of Moloch, because gods thus conceived seemed to offer more immediate satisfaction for their primal lusts. The prophet Samuel interpreted the God of Israel as a God of such terrific vengeance that he could order the utter slaughter of the Amalekites after they had been overcome in war; and one of the psalmists could regard with such exultancy the extermination of his people's foes that he could cry in regard to Babylon, "Blessed shall he be that taketh thy children and throweth them against the stones." [2] When Jesus came to Galilee he came into the midst of a people almost fanatically religious; but to the minds of most of them God had become a kind of private deity concerned merely with the fortunes of a particular nation, and

[2] Psalm 137:9, Prayer-Book version.

honored by a religion of formalized conventions and codes. When we ask, therefore, whether Christians can believe in a God above this human life of ours, we must know first what sort of God we mean.

The answer, of course, if the answer is to be worth establishing, is the God whom Jesus called his "Father."

But here we come to the difficulty of that second group of people to whom we have referred. Is the God whom Jesus believed in real? Or is the One in whom he trusted, and in whom men would like to trust today, only an infinite mirage?

Middleton Murry, the well-known English literary critic, has thrust this thought forward with exceptional sharpness in his *Things to Come*. Referring to Jesus' death on Calvary he wrote:

Jesus "created God the Father. Created Him; and believed in him steadily, unflinchingly, all his life. . . . He would trust God the Father to the uttermost, to show men the way to trust Him. He trusted Him; he died in agony; and his last words were: 'My God, my God, why hast thou forsaken me?'

"His God, the good God, the loving God, the Father Almighty, did not exist. Jesus died knowing it. No pain in the world of men has ever been like that pain. . . .

"Men would *like* to trust God as a Father, no doubt. I know well enough the hunger of the human soul for a Father who cares. But we cannot have all we long for.

And which is better: to half-believe in a loving Father who does not exist, or to believe wholly in a loving Son who did?" [3]

There is the problem posed unmistakably. Is the only God which Christians can have the God which they have made for themselves in Jesus? And is it only an understandable, but nevertheless in the end a weak and futile wishful-thinking, that makes men try to believe in a transcendent Father who does not now and never did exist?

So we are brought face to face with the question which undoubtedly has made its uneasy presence felt in the midst of the themes of the earlier chapters. Can we honestly believe today in God; and more particularly can we believe in the sort of God whom the New Testamen reveals as the ground of the faith of Jesus? Obviously, this is the crucial point in any proclamation of a Christian gospel. There can be no gospel, no confident "good news," unless it be true that there is an answer to man's everlasting cry, "O that I knew where I might find *Him*."

Let us begin, then, by exploring the faith of Jesus, as to the validity of which Middleton Murry makes so summary a denial.

Of *this* certainly there can be no question: the rela-

[3] Pp. 101, 102, 103. By permission of Jonathan Cape, Ltd., London, and The Macmillan Company.

tionship which Jesus *believed* he had with the one whom he called his Father did create in him a life which is generally recognized as the finest flowering of our humanity. It did give him his power to dare and to endure and to move through all adverse circumstances not only with courage but with an amazing sort of joy.

It is a striking fact that Jesus never argued about God. He never put his disciples through a course of reasoning as to why they should believe in Him as God. He led them to explore ways in which they might find God. Exploration is always better than speculation. If men do grow conscious that they are finding God, then they do not have to go back and argue whether He was there for them to find.

Jesus' own assurance of God was based upon the vital certainty with which he felt his own personality to be companioned by Another as he held his spirit sensitive to life. He communicated faith in God to his disciples simply by letting them see the power of that spontaneous faith in him. With little need of words he made plain his living consciousness that, back of this seen world, there is a spiritual Reality with whom the soul can come into contact by prayer and communion in such wise as to receive direction for the conscience, purification for the will, and strength and confidence both for the near duties of the day and for life's far destinies. This communion of his soul with God was an orientation of his whole life, a swinging of every faculty toward an immense focus of assurance, as the compass needle swings toward the pole. The witness to this begins with the one convincing glimpse which tradition has saved of his boyhood—of that visit to Jerusalem, when with a beautiful astonishment, he replied to his mother's question as to why he had gone to the Temple with a question of his own, "Wist ye not that I must be in my Father's house?" [4] This same sense of God shines from him through all the story of the Synoptic Gospels. He speaks as one who had authority; he bears himself as one who had authority; and that authority was God. He treats the sick and the afflicted as though divine power were at his disposal. He faces the growing circle of his enemies with an intrepid confidence which came from the fact that he believed the divine resources could outmatch all human resistance and gainsaying. At the end he goes up to Jerusalem, ready if need be to die, and through death to carry the torch of his high faith that not even death itself could defeat the life which had put its trust in God.

The great phrase which rang continually on the lips of Jesus was "the Kingdom of God." Volumes have been written and will yet be written on what the Kingdom meant to Jesus. Did he share the apocalyptic expectations of his contemporaries? Did he hope that the Kingdom would come swiftly with some tremendous miracle of opened heavens and descending legions of

[4] Luke 2:49.

angelic hosts? Did he believe, when he faced his cross, that he would never actually be allowed to die, or that, if he did die, he would immediately return throned on the clouds of heaven? Or did he foresee the fact that the coming of the Kingdom would be a long and silent thing, and was this what he meant by his parables of the leaven and of the mustard seed? We cannot clearly tell. But one thing we can tell, namely, that the Kingdom, whenever and however it might come, was the Kingdom *of God*. No human contrivance could bring it in. It depended upon the will of the one upon whom Jesus utterly relied, and whom he called for himself, and taught his disciples to call, the Father. He believed that what men could not do, God could do, and would, if He could find souls obedient to His purpose. He believed that the spiritual energies of God are transcendent facts, mightily existent, superbly available to accomplish in human life what that life in its uninspired dullness would not dare to dream.

But the Kingdom, though a gift of God, must be received by men. It must show itself in lives transformed by a new relationship to God. It should work as salt, and light, and leaven.

The unqualified confidence which Jesus had in God, and in His strong assurance, worked in him an unexampled consciousness of power. It so released and unified the energies of his spirit that he could exert a control beyond all ordinary limits upon the physical as well as the

spiritual natures of men. He felt himself to be the
ambassador of a Kingdom which no mortal might could
stay; and with a splendor of imagination which sometimes required language like that of the apocalypses for
its expression, he foresaw the Kingdom's victory.

Meanwhile it is important to remember that in his
own thought of God and in what he said of God to
others Jesus was not in bondage to tradition. He definitely set aside many of the teachings of his forerunners about God. The fact that men said thus and
thus of old time was no barrier to the freedom of his
new interpretations. He spoke the language which men
of his own generation understood. If he were living in
this generation and in this modern world, he would
speak with the same accents of certainty which he had
long ago, but he would use another terminology. He
would relate his conviction of God to the horizon of
contemporary thinking with the same creative freshness
that was his in that day when his hearers moved in a
smaller orbit than that in which men are moving now.

Moreover, it is significant that Jesus characteristically
saw God not in the occasional but in the usual. This is
one of the ways in which he was so great that his interpreters have mostly half understood and often wholly
misrepresented him. The natural tendency of the ordinary man is to go on his humdrum way, thinking
very little about God, and imagining that, if God comes
into his life at all, it will be through some startling and

extraordinary happening. In order for God to be manifest, there must be a miracle. There must come, just as
the old prophet Elijah thought, earthquakes and thun-
ders and lightnings, if God is really moving. To most
people it never occurs that God's real way of speaking
is, as it was to Elijah, through the still small voice. But
Jesus knew that. His soul was so sensitive to the divine
meaning in common things that the voice of God was
speaking to him continually. It spoke to him from the
lilies growing in the fields, from birds nesting in the
hedgerows, from sheep coming home at eventide, from
all the pathos and beauty and homely courage of the
daily life of people round him,—from the woman
kneading bread, from the shepherd looking for his lost
lamb, from the sower planting his grain in the field.
To his eyes the whole universe was alive, alive together
with something infinite and beneficent which day by day
revealed its beauty and its orderliness of truth.

So Jesus linked his message of God with the actual
test of everyday existence. He did not point to the past
only, but to the present. He built religion, not upon a
legend, but upon its results in life. It was as though he
asked—and says: "Is the world today alive, or not?
Is there a Spirit with whom the souls of men can come
into communion, or not? How shall you know? The
only way is to trust and try the intuition that whispers
within your soul. Act as though that strange quivering
consciousness of God is true. Let the thought of it

penetrate your thought; let the power of it possess your imagination; and you will see whether or not God proves Himself to you. All the elements of life will swing into their places round a central peace. Venture upon God, and the increasing power and certainty of your living will be the vindication of your faith."

Now it would be disingenuous to suggest that there are not difficulties in the way of accepting Jesus' representation of God, for there are. There are difficulties both in reconciling his faith with the facts of his own life, and also in adopting his faith for the life of today. But the existence of difficulties does not mean that there is no way through.

Suppose it be suggested, and suppose it be granted, that Jesus probably thought of God's relation to what is now called "the order of nature" in a way which, in certain respects at least, would be impossible to the thinking of the present day. Born into the world at a particular time—and inheriting, as he must have done to be human —those general conceptions of the physical world which were universal in that day, he could not have felt, as we do, those rigid preconceptions of regularity in the natural order which modern science—or shall we now say slightly pre-modern science?—has ingrained into this generation. He may have had no doubt that his Father might at any moment accomplish by immediate and heavenly intervention anything which needed to be done to make His spiritual purposes prevail. It may have been in an unqualified sense that he believed that God was Lord of heaven and earth, and that all things were possible for His accomplishment.

But we should err if we did not hold through all our thought of Jesus the remembrance that in him there was a great creative intellect. It is true that his thought must have moved within the general framework of knowledge possible to his time; but within that framework he was not passive. He was reshaping and revaluing the ideas which he inherited in the light of the facts which his clear eyes perceived. As he meditated upon the history of his people, as he watched men's destinies unfolding in the world around him, and as he pondered the interplay of his own desires and the stubborn facts of the environment with which he had to reckon, he seems to have become increasingly aware that, whatever might be the *a priori* possibilities, yet in actual experience God does not work in sudden and ejaculatory fashion. If ever he relied upon it in the beginning, apparently less and less as his life went on did he rely upon what is commonly called miracle but trusted instead to deeper and slower movements which represent the permeation of this world by the power of God. With the miracle stories as they stand in the New Testament, there is not time individually to deal. Many of them represent an original nucleus of fact which has become invested with magnifying atmosphere of tradition. But even as the tradition stands, it is a striking fact that the Evangelists, implicitly as they believed in the actuality of miracles, have at the same time conveyed the impression of Jesus as reluctant to emphasize them or to use them as credentials of his ministry. Very significant also is the record of the temptation in the wilderness, with the profound suggestion which it gives of a definite turning away of Jesus' mind from anything violent or startling and his adoption instead of a conception of the will of God which deliberately sacrificed the dramatic, and dared venture everything upon the power of self-denying love as the only thing that could work redemption.

Moreover, as Jesus' life went on, two things which superficially seemed incongruous, but ultimately were not so, appear to have happened in his consciousness. On the one hand, he came to feel that there might be facts in the world, both physical and moral, which for the time were intractable to that love which he worshipped as his Father. It *may* be true, as many critics believe, that he hoped to the end for an immediate deliverance, hoped that the hands of God out of heaven would snatch him from the death of the cross, or, after the moment of death, send him swiftly back clothed in the messianic transfiguration of heaven. But the truth may be instead that by the end of his life, if not at the beginning, the immeasurable religious genius of Jesus had perceived that the nature of God and the process of redemption were at once more inward and more infinite than had ever been dreamed before. Even the acceptance of his death did not dim his confidence in the triumph of his Father's purpose. In the time to come, through ways that might not be catastrophic but should be no less certain, the love of God, by which he had lived and from which he had drawn his strength, would create the growing Kingdom of its redemption in the lives of men. If this be true, it must plainly follow, therefore, that Middleton Murry is wrong when he writes of Jesus as having died in agony, "knowing that the Father whom he worshipped did not exist." He died in physical agony; yes. In spiritual agony; no. There is no valid reason for assuming, as Middleton Murry does, that *"My God, my God, why hast thou forsaken me?"* [5] were the last words on the cross, nor, even if they were, that they represented only a bitter outcry of despair. Those words on the lips of Jesus were an echo from the psalms, and the psalm which they introduce moves on to its climax of victory. Nor in any case is there sufficient reason for ignoring the further tradition which the Gospel of Luke has preserved. Some New Testament criticism questions the objective accuracy of all the words of Jesus on the cross. As one of the ablest of contemporary scholars has put it: "All the words from the cross are the creation of the early Church. Jesus uttered a sharp inarticulate cry which

[5] Mark 15:34.

tradition filled out variously." [6] To many this will seem too sweeping a statement; but whether it be accepted or not accepted, in either case the stress which Middleton Murry lays upon one particular reported word of Jesus is discredited. If we do not know exactly what Jesus said, then it is impossible to draw the dogmatic conclusion which Murry draws from one reported cry; but if the traditions are held to be authentic, as Christian opinion in the main has held, then the traditions which Luke preserves must be set alongside the cry of *"My God, my God, why hast thou forsaken me?"* Luke is in curiously repeated instances the Gospel of the women, and it is reasonable to suppose that, from the women, who were nearest to the foot of the cross, those other sayings should have been authentically reported which Luke in his Gospel has written down: the promise to the repentant thief: *"Today shalt thou be with me in paradise,"* [7] and the last great cry to God, *"Father, into thy hands I commend my spirit."* [8]

Yet the question can be pressed: How can we go on believing that a God of love exists, or that, if He does exist, His effect upon the world is of any practical consequence, when we are faced with the fact that the Father whom Jesus called upon did let him die upon the cross, and that the heavenly love, if such there be, does constantly let human beings suffer and agonize today?

[6] Burton S. Easton, D.D., Professor of the Literature and Interpretation of the New Testament in the General Theological Seminary, New York, in a letter to the author.

[7] Luke 23:43.　　　　　[8] Luke 23:46.

To that question there is not, and never has been, any absolute answer. Philosophers, metaphysicians, wrestlers with the ultimate problems of the intellect all are baffled by the contradiction which seems to exist between belief in sovereign Goodness and the existence in the world of so much that is not good; between the postulate of love omnipotent and the fact of evil and of darkness. Theoretically there is no way of solving the enigma.

But practically there is. The whole history of religion presents the paradox that evil can be transmuted into good; and more—that what seems evil may often be the condition out of which the most transcendent good will take its rise. However strange it be, it is nevertheless true that not in spite of the cross but through the cross men in all the ages since have been most touched by a revealing grace which made them believe in God. Jesus, in what has seemed to critics like Middleton Murry the hour of his faith's defeat, was not defeated; and from that hour faith in the God who can be trusted through every darkness, instead of being defeated, has been born anew. It is not most of all the Jesus of sunny Galilee, but the Jesus crucified, who has become to men a savior. And one of the great world-figures of our generation, Cardinal Mercier, a spiritual warrior-saint, said as he lay dying of cancer after a life which had had in it much tragedy as well as much heroism: "Physical pain is such a petty thing.[9] . . . I

[9] *The Life of Cardinal Mercier,* by John A. Gade, p. 282.

am content, very content. I thank the good Lord for having permitted me to follow Him, at least part of the way towards Calvary and to have suffered on the Cross. Suffering—that is the complete apostleship." [10]

This then is the Christian gospel of God as it is learned from Jesus: that above all life's confusing and obscuring lesser facts there does rise the great Fact; that not by intellectual calculations nor by any dogmatics but by the discovery of souls in action that Fact may be possessed; that it is known not by any finalities of reasoning but by the fertility which it brings to life; and that because of it all the foregrounds and all the backgrounds of our destiny are seen to be brooded over by the Divine.

Let us pass on then beyond the phase of discussion as to whether God exists. If He did not exist, it is certain that discussion would not create Him. Existent, He has no need of our discussion to give Him permission to be alive. Our human business is to see what happens when we try to relate ourselves to the Reality which great souls in every age who have sought for Him have declared to be *there*. As William Adams Brown has nobly put it, "God makes His presence known with irresistible conviction in the act of will by which man surrenders without reserve to the highest he knows.[11]

[10] *Ibid.*, p. 285.   [11] *God at Work*, p. 118.

"To surrender without reserve to the highest he knows" requires of course a venture of faith. A man may say that the highest he glimpses is not *a* highest he *knows;* it may be only something he hopes and wishes for so much that he is persuading himself that it is true. His mood may be like that expressed in a letter which a certain minister received. The young person who wrote it, after having been part of a group which both in thought and life were wholly irreligious, came almost by chance into a contact which waked in her a sudden wistful sense of what the life in God might mean, yet left her irresolute because of her doubt that God could be. She wrote:

"I wish you would say: 'I don't believe in God, but I preach about him, and write about him, and talk about him, because it helps people. It brings something into their lives, one way or another, and they're the better for it. It gives them peace and happiness, and in their turn they will hand that on, so certainly no one is any the worse for it. But what I really think is that man, even though happy and busy and surrounded by people, has moments of loneliness that nothing in the world satisfies, and so, out of his need, which he doesn't quite understand, he has, through the ages, created a God. But it's really just a charming fairy tale. God didn't create man—man created God.'

"But of course you won't say that. First of all because for you it wouldn't be true—and if it were you could hardly say so. But I wish you would, because it would let me go.

"I don't believe what you say, although I like to hear you say it. Once or twice I wondered if it could be true, and more than that, thought it possible that it might be true. Then I laugh at myself and resolve never to go to the church again. Nobody is making me go but myself. But even though I laugh, I go back—and it's a merry-go-round.

"I want to talk with you, and the reason is this. Sometime ago I made up my mind that there were two courses. One to go on seeing and appreciating all the lovely things in the world for what they are, with nothing more back of them than just that. Or the other, to accept the creed of the worldly-wise people I know, the creed of materialism and sophistry, and the belief that, because it can buy so much, money is all powerful. And then the thing I have been listening to catapulted across the horizon. So here I am, and I can't be a peaceful pagan or a happy materialist. And it's very uncomfortable."

"It's very uncomfortable." That is the way a life which has not found God is bound to feel. It is moving erratically in a universe which seems to have no steadying significance. It does not dare to trust its own best intuitions, because it is browbeaten by a materialism which makes a mockery of these. But then to such a life may come somehow and from somewhere a voice that says to it—"Make the venture! You cannot respond to human friendship if you hang back and refuse to trust its possibility. Neither can you respond to the infinite Friend if you refuse to listen to the message that is trembling in your heart. Act as though your half-belief must lead on to the whole. Listen to the voices of the spirit, and let your whole personality be open to the assurances they bring!"

In the first place let God speak through beauty. Thus did Jesus. He looked at the lilies in the Galilean fields, he watched the birds as they built their nests, he saw the light in little children's eyes, and the loveliness he found in homely things like these seemed to him no superficial accident; it brought to him a sense of One who had made it all, and with whom therefore all human joy in beauty could feel itself attuned.

It is possible for all to find, as he did, in every thing of beauty the mystic chalice of a divine assurance, and to drink from it the draught of joy. There is no need that men and women should be inhibited from an instinctive religious faith by the fact that they cannot prove that beauty has any divine significance. In their deepest moments of appreciation they *feel* that it has; and their best wisdom is to follow this feeling, and see to what further conviction it may lead on.

Suppose, however, that one should ask, "But what is beauty?" and should demonstrate that this is a question

difficult to answer. Standards of beauty, and verdicts as
to what men call beautiful, seem to vary strangely from
age to age. Our so-called modern art is to many of its
votaries beautiful, but to many others it appears to be
a delirium through which our contemporary generation
is passing, and to which some day it will look back with
incredulity, as a man looks back upon a disordered
dream. Nevertheless, beneath the changing fashions,
there are certain great recognitions which abide, and
which forever are the norms by which our vagrant
tastes are judged. Always we know the beauty of a sunrise, or of a starlit winter sky, or of a mountain lifted
to the blue. We recognize the ageless beauty of the
Parthenon, or the white loveliness of the Taj Mahal.
And when men enjoy, or more especially when they
create, great beauty, they do not feel that they are having an accidental experience. Neither do they feel as
though they were tasting a mere shallow pleasure which
welled up from within. The great lovers of beauty, and
the great artists, feel that their inspiration comes to
them from something which is eternal and other than
themselves. Rightly we speak of the supreme art, or
music, or poetry, as *inspired*. That word expresses the
age-old conviction that beauty in the human apprehension has been breathed from something more than human, the fire of genius kindled by the flames which come
from God.

But it is not alone, nor most significantly, in that

145

beauty which genius recognizes that beauty can convey its sense of the divine. To everyday men and women, gifted with no more than ordinary awareness, there can come, and does come, an emotion in the presence of beauty which is more than sensory. It is not only with the eye or the ear that they perceive; an instinct in their souls responds to a deeper and more mystic something which is present in that which they see as beautiful.

Such is the truth concerning beauty, put in general terms. But who is there that cannot make it definite out of his own remembrance? Rare is the man who does not possess somewhere in his mind the picture of an old or new beauty which has moved him. He has had his moments when he stood possessed by something which lifted him out of himself—out of his humdrum self into a larger self that breathed a quickening air. It may have been any one of the familiar miracles of this familiar earth that moved him:—the glory of sunrise breaking across a dewy hill, the smell of hay and of clover as the sun climbs high, the stillness of wide fields where cow-bells tinkle and the shadows of elm-trees lengthen as the evening falls, the silver silence of moonlight on still waters, the blue of distant mountains carved against a winter sky, the foaming of the sea against a rocky shore, the majesty of ascending stars. Or the thing of beauty may be more intimate than these—the first shy arbutus of the spring, the flash of a bluebird in the orchard, the glint of sunlight on the hair of a little child in the doorway of an old gray house. All these are more than sight or sound. They set deep bells of the spirit ringing. They may for an instant make the heart almost stop beating with a sense of something over-powering, as though one had suddenly stepped through the shell of things and touched Reality, in wonder, and mystery, and awe.

It is the function of religious interpreters to help men and women recognize more explicitly this sense of the Infinite which is implicit in their own experience, to feel more confidently and steadily what they sometimes shyly grasp at and then let go, to know that for them as well as for the poet it can be true that forever in its humblest aspects beauty, and the appreciation of it, can bring God close to human life. Early on a Sunday morning at the beginning of spring, a man was passing through one of the east-side tenement streets of the city of New York. Because it was Sunday and because it was early the street was very still, and almost empty. But as he walked between the drab and unlovely houses, he saw ahead of him a tiny negro boy. The child could hardly have been more than five years old. He was exceedingly bow-legged, so that the small figure of him was ludicrously outlined to the one who came behind. He had evidently been sent to the corner grocery store to buy a loaf of bread. This loaf of bread he held tucked to his left shoulder, as though he had a violin, while in his right hand he had a green switch with which he was bowing the imagined violin with as much abandon as though it were a Stradivarius; while at the same time he sang a song of his own invention at the top of his small lungs. Then to the one who watched him and listened to him, the whole shabby street was suddenly transfigured. For in that small child's heart was the instinctive love of beauty which everywhere can bring a divine fire to this earth. Through him and through what he longed for, and through what in his childish way he sought to be, the word of God which can be "very nigh thee, in thy mouth, and in thy heart" was drawing near.

A second way in which men become aware of God is through the search for truth, especially in its aspect as a search for *meaning*. There is a search for truth which is independent of the desire for meaning. The explorations of the scientists are directed toward discovering what is. They try to learn more and more completely what the objective facts of this universe may be. Whether or not these may ultimately be seen to be integrated into any intelligible purpose is not the scientist's main concern. Indeed for the pure scientist it is not primarily his concern even to ask for what purpose, good or bad, man may use what he discovers. The physicist, delving into the nature and composition of the atom, is not turned this way or that in his conclusions by a desire to harmonize his facts with a moral philosophy for the universe. Neither will he cease in his efforts to unlock the energy in the atom because of the very genuine possibility that men might use that power, if they had it, in hideous ways. The business of the scientist, when he is most true to his own profession, is to analyze and to describe with utmost accuracy and completeness the raw materials of this universe; and it is the business of some one else to study whether, through the elements and energies thus revealed, there can be traced some mighty Purpose which from the aspect of living souls gives this universe significance.

Sometimes of course scientists may overpass the boundaries within which their method is authoritative. They may essay to be philosophers, and philosophers of negation. Because their test tubes and balances cannot weigh or measure purpose, they may announce that this universe is nothing but matter and blind chance. But always then man's instinct for a larger meaning, which is the instinct for religion, pursues its search upon a larger ground. As an able modern Rabbi has written:

"A scientific age, reared in materialism, may and frequently does, become a pessimistic age. A materialistic metaphysics leads first to stoicism and then to cynicism and finally to despair. Our modern pessimism is based not on the belief that knowledge will not increase, but on the belief that increased knowledge will bring us decreased happiness, nobility, and self-esteem. A trayful of mechanical toys, of engines and motors and radios and airplanes, is no adequate compensation for the irrevocable loss of idealism and hope and human pride." [12]

Idealism and hope and human pride would dwindle and disappear if men came increasingly to believe that the life they live is ultimately meaningless. The desire for integration is the instinct for the preservation of life itself, and that instinct therefore reaches out constantly toward religion. For many people today life is like the pieces of an intricate picture puzzle strewn indiscriminately on the table. Laboriously one may find two or three pieces which obviously fit together. At least those few fragments give some sign of belonging to a wholeness that will make sense. Yonder two or three other odd and crooked curves and angles may also interlock. But the picture will not begin to grow surely until some clue to its whole pattern begins to be glimpsed. Here it is discovered, perhaps, that all the pieces of this particular blue are the blue of a river. Those greens belong to a field, and those deeper greens to a forest. That deeper blue is of hills upon the horizon. And that seeming confusion of other colors is revealed to be the sunrise sky. When this is seen, then the whole pattern becomes an encouragement and a guide by which the many pieces of the puzzle more quickly and certainly take shape. And some such result as this is what men and

[12] *Religion in a Changing World,* by Rabbi Abba Hillel Silver, p. 13. By permission of Harper & Brothers.

women search for in their lives. So much of life seems to be made of disconnected trivialities; so much of it is a jumble of meaningless incidents that seem to link with nothing else. Here and there some obvious necessity does interlock with another necessity, and one knows that in that incident at least life has some logical sureness. Here and there one duty draws to itself another duty, and those two things, so far as they go at least, are indisputable. But what of the pattern of the whole? Now and then there seems to be a clue to it. Is the clue real and can we trust it? That is what we want to know. Is there really a river of refreshment of the love of God running past the fields where our ordinary daily work is done? Are there on the horizon hills of hope and aspiration to which we may lift our eyes forever and be glad? Is there above us the immensity of the sky, filled with the rushing splendor of the morning? Is earth over-arched by the high heaven of the infinite in which the light of God forever shines? If so, then all our existence here begins to be beautiful and full of meaning. The broken pieces fall into place in the great pattern under which the growing life finds its unity in God.

The search for truth which religion motivates must not conflict with the search of science. It should illuminate it with a larger interpretation—an interpretation born not of part of the human personality but of the whole. Science does not ask questions about the ends of life. Religion is bound to do so. And the conviction of religion is that as men do study the discovered facts of nature in connection with their own purposive instinct as to life's highest and noblest ends, they find that the great trends of nature are friendly to those ends, and in that friendliness they find themselves in touch with God.

This communion with God through the search for truth conceived as *meaning* has been clearly expressed by Professor Arthur H. Compton, winner of one of the Nobel Prize awards for physics, in a brief declaration of his own belief made in 1933 on Christmas Day. He wrote:

"Science can have no quarrel with a religion which postulates a God to whom men are as His children. Not that science in any way shows such a relationship. If a religion which makes such an assumption does not have its own evidence, it should not look to science. But the evidence for an intelligent power working in the world which science offers does make such a postulate plausible.

"It is thus possible to see the whole great drama of evolution as moving toward the goal of personality, the making of persons with free, intelligent wills, capable of learning nature's laws, of glimpsing God's purpose in nature and of sharing that purpose.

"It is an inspiring setting in which we thus find ourselves. As we recognize the greatness of the program of nature which is unfolding before us we feel that we are part of a great enterprise in which some mighty intelligence is working out a hidden plan.

"Indeed, God has placed us in a position to help in furthering his program. For do we not hold in our hands and control the conditions of vegetable and animal life on this planet, and, to some extent, human life?" [13]

In the same mood is a passage from the autobiography of Edwin Brant Frost, for many years the director of the Yerkes Observatory, entitled *An Astronomer's Life*.

"Everything that we learn from the observational point of view in the study of astronomy," he writes, "seems to me to point precisely and always toward a purposeful operation of nature. When you accept this, it seems to me inconsistent with physical science not to believe in a mind behind the universe. . . . If the universe is purposeful then it is plain to me that man, who is the highest form of development on the earth, must himself be distinctly a result of purpose rather than of accident. . . . One thing illustrative of this spiritual attitude is that man has his curiosities, his wonder, his awe and his reverence for the material universe he sees about him, which may indicate to him a divine purpose behind it."

And not less significant than what Professor Frost

[13] "Compton Holds Faith in God Is Scientific." By permission of *The New York Times*.

has written is the effect of his personality in carrying authentication of what his words express. In *The New York Times Book Review* of June 30, 1932, is a long summary of the book, and a final reference to this sentence of Professor Frost, "I believe that the more we ... look at matter from the cosmic point of view, the more will the great things of God become greater and the small things of life will become smaller." Whereupon, the reviewer goes on to say: "Perhaps it was in this philosophy that Mr. Frost found the grace to endure so equably the affliction of blindness that came upon him within recent years. He tells with staunch and serene spirit of the salvages he has made from what to many another would have been a wreckage of life." [14]

And also this reviewer sets down a comment which may well serve as a concluding word upon the theme which we have been developing, namely, that it is the values being wrought out in human spirits that afford the divine meaning in the light of which the realities of this universe are read:

" 'To be is better than to achieve.' This ancient truth is once more exemplified in this modest autobiography of an eminent astronomer. Mr. Frost's achievements in his special branch of astronomy, astrophysics, have been important and have helped to push forward

[14] From a review by Florence Finch Heeley in *The New York Times* of *An Astronomer's Life,* by Edwin Brant Frost.

the frontiers of science, but as one follows the simple, wholesome story of his life the conviction is born and grows in the reader's mind that no matter what were his achievements the man himself has been of greater consequence to humanity than what he did." [15]

The thought suggested here is a bridge by which we pass over to our next consideration. We have contemplated the ways in which the awareness of beauty and the desire for truth may lead to the recognition of an Infinite which lies around and above our human consciousness. But the religious instinct cannot stop with the "recognition of an Infinite"; it reached on to feel itself in living touch with the living God. And for this to be fully achieved, a life must move upon the plane where it becomes true, as in the comment made upon the great astronomer, that the man himself is of more consequence than even the utmost that he does. In other words, it is in a man's whole response to the wholeness of life that he becomes aware of God. Beauty reveals one aspect of God; truth reveals another; but it is nothing less than the whole complex of existence, sensitively perceived, honestly regarded, and *bravely dealt with,* which can convey to a man the unshakeable sense of a Soul companioning his soul. He must live religiously if he would have and hold religion.

The theorist will be swift here with his protest.

[15] *Ibid.*

"What cart-before-the-horse-logic is this?" he will object. "Why talk of practising a conviction which you have not gained? If you are going to live religiously, certainly you must have had religion proved to you first," he will say.

But the reality of life is different. The living convictions spring not from antecedent proof; they spring from instincts which, like little seeds, carry upon the face of them no sign of their great unfolding, but which do unfold through the sun and rain of everyday experience. To be sure of God, men must plant those elements of themselves which are of God in the ground of common faithfulness. Then by that which blossoms they will know the meaning of the divine.

Such has been the experience of religion in all generations. Men have found God most certainly not through their ideas but through their ideals. As they have tried to be good, they have been conscious of the Goodness which created and undergirded whatever was good in them. They have felt God most when most they were trying to fulfil themselves. And this fact of experience is what the clearest thinking comes presently to see as being exactly what might have been expected. For God, if He is all that men have desired, must be what we mean by personality. That is to say, He must certainly have in Himself, as distinguished from unconscious matter and from unmeaning force, the spiritual creativeness, with its capacity to think, to wonder, to will and to love, which makes man creative in his own sphere. Or if "personality" in our limited human sense seems too finite a word to use of God, and if there should be ascribed to Him a "super-personality," then not the less but all the more must it be true that only when man extends himself to the highest and widest in his own nature does he come most into touch with God. That is why so many people who have not been able to explain God to others have nevertheless been sure of Him themselves; yes, and why people whose own thoughts of God have been crude and imperfect have nevertheless lived in the power of His life. And that also is why some who have been very orthodox in their opinions have lacked any divine fire in what they called their religion. They have never discovered the infinite life because they themselves were living churlishly. They were jealous, or proud, or selfish, or vindictive. They were damming life back instead of letting it go out. They were shutting their personalities into self-absorption and self-seeking instead of letting them expand in sympathy and good-will. So, because they sinned against the cardinal principle of life, they could not know Him in whom all life centers. Whereas, on the contrary, even simple and otherwise very imperfect folk, who yet have been ready to live expansively, have been witnesses in every generation to contact with a power greater than the energies of this earth.

It is here that a book like the Old Testament can be

so inspiring; for it is starred with the record of those who revealed in action the reality of God.

Take, for example, the story of Joseph. He appears first as a lad full of ambition and imagination. He dreams his golden dreams of greatness. Boyishly self-absorbed and unmindful of others were those dreams at first. He was to be exalted and his brothers were to bow down. There was a great deal he had to learn if he was to adjust himself to life. But one supreme secret of ultimate power he did possess. He believed that life must essentially be noble. He insisted that his own destiny need be no common thing.

And in no common way, therefore, did he bear himself. His envious and disgusted brothers sold him as a slave into Egypt, and told their father that he was dead. There in Egypt he descended through one disaster into another. He was lied against and punished, not because of anything wrong that he had done but rather because of his very decency which provoked vindictiveness against him. He was not only a slave now but a convict in a common jail. Nevertheless, his sense of high destiny, and the obligation of faithfulness which went with it, never left him. In a moment of moral crisis he had said: "How can I do this great wickedness, and sin against God?" [16] And in the prison, he believed that God was with him still.

Then follows in the story the dramatic account of

[16] Genesis 29:9.

Joseph's rise to greatness. In the prison, he befriends another prisoner. Through that prisoner, Joseph is released, brought to the knowledge of the Pharaoh under circumstances which made Joseph render to Pharaoh a service that nobody else could give. Then presently Joseph is raised to the vice-royalty in Egypt. He is in command of all the stored-up grain upon which the nation must depend through years of famine. And then down into Egypt and into the presence of their long-vanished and unrecognized brother come Joseph's own brothers, pleading for permission to buy food; and when one day they learn that this man who holds over them the power of life and death is Joseph, they shrink back in terror. But in that moment of his ascendancy, turning from all thought of vengeance, Joseph summed up into one expression the consciousness which had given power to all his life and which stood vindicated now as his life's reliance. "Be not grieved, nor angry with yourselves, that ye sold me hither: for God did send me before you to preserve life. . . . So now it was not you that sent me hither, but God." [17]

Or turn to the other figures of which the Old Testament tells. There is Moses, finding in his trust in God the power and patience to lead a people out of slavery into freedom, and of whom long afterward it was magnificently to be written that "he endured, as seeing him who is invisible." [18] There is David, a man most fully

[17] Genesis 45 :5, 8.   [18] Hebrews 11 :27.

human in his imperfections and his passions, yet lifted into greatness because he felt himself accountable to something greater and higher than himself. There is Elijah, lonely and intrepid, confronting a king with a moral power that overrode any majesty the king could muster, fearing the face of no man because his own face was lighted by the awful authority which came from his sense of communion with the living God. There is Nehemiah, believing that he was about God's business when he was rebuilding the walls of destroyed Jerusalem and saying to them who tried to stop him, "I am doing a great work. . . . Why should the work cease, whilst I leave it, and come down to you?" [19] And loftiest of all, there are the towering figures of the later prophets who, following in the footsteps of Elijah, became the consciences of their time, and who were so sure of their own contact with the Infinite that when they spoke they dared to say, "Thus saith the Lord!"

But of course it is not necessary to go back to such distant years for examples of men who in their living made God plain. There is Paul saying before Agrippa, "Whereupon I was not disobedient unto the heavenly vision." [20] There is Savonarola dying in the market place at Florence for the truth he dared proclaim. There is Martin Luther crying, "Here I stand. God help me, I cannot do otherwise." And in this present time there has been a shining representative of the

[19] Nehemiah 6:3.   [20] Acts 26:19.

immediate power which the sense of oneness with God can give to a human personality. Words of the great Cardinal of Belgium, Désiré Joseph Mercier, have been quoted earlier in this chapter; but here is what was said not by him but about him by one who had been his enemy. During the World War, when Belgium was occupied by the invaders, the aide to the German Governor-General was Baron von der Lancken, and to von der Lancken fell the task of carrying to the Cardinal again and again those demands and threats by which the occupying power tried in vain to silence his intrepid voice. After the war, in a German paper, von der Lancken wrote:

"Certainly no one has fought the Germans with sharper weapons than did Mercier; certainly no one has done us more harm in Belgium and throughout the world. . . . But he had no bitter hatred for Germany. Apart from his religious duties, which he had very much at heart, he was far too intelligent to hate, and he would not have been so dangerous to us as he became, if his patriotism had been stimulated by the impulse of hatred. He fought us with invincible strength and pitiless dialectics, which he had acquired by the long discipline of his will, of his spirit, and of his whole personality. He was dangerous to us owing to the spiritual ascendancy and the sovereign prestige which these characteristics gave him." [21]

And if one asks for the secret of the "spiritual

[21] *The Life of Cardinal Mercier,* by John A. Gade, p. 191.

ascendancy" which this man possessed, the answer is in the words which Mercier himself once spoke concerning what at the beginning of his life his mother taught him—"It was in her heart, in the serene virility of her resolutions, that I first read the great lesson of life: That man is nothing, that success and adversity are nothing, that God alone matters." [22]

It is the business of men in the ministry to communicate to others this truth "that God alone matters," and the man who has himself found God and been found by Him can do it. As I write this, I think of a certain evening when I listened to three young men talking together about religion. One of them was in the ministry. Of the other two, one had just graduated from college, and the third was an undergraduate. These two had read widely among those modern books which not only cast doubt on particular religious convictions but invest all the outlines of life with a fog of pessimism and near despair, until many of the present generation believe that no landmarks of conviction are stable any more. The first man was not so widely read as either of the others, nor had his educational advantages been so thorough. He had stopped college in the middle of his course to enlist as a private in the war, had seen service in France, then gone into business for a time. In the beginning of the discussion, it seemed

[22] *Ibid.*, p. 3.

as though the others had the weight of the argument on their side. They were ready with ideas and quotations; but little by little it became evident that what they knew was disjointed. It was made up of many miscellaneous items of hearsay, debate, and academic speculation which had never been bound together by any strong, clear feeling which could result in conclusions authoritative and sure. The other man by contrast may have known less than they; but what he knew, he knew far better. He was concerned with people and not with ideas only. In his own relationships first— his loyalty to those he loved and who loved him, his steadfastness to his friends and his readiness to show friendship to those who had no claim upon him—he was always binding the things he knew and the things he thought into a principle of living. He had a sure instinct which made him know that ultimately the only sound ideas are those which set the whole personality free. He had no false vanity in knowledge for itself, nor did he ever make pretense to a knowledge which he did not have; but he could not speak a word before you knew that here was one whose intellectual grasp was cleancut and sure. He did not merely possess casual opinions and toss them into the air as a juggler tosses glass balls to reveal his own dexterity. He had convictions that were warm with living fire, a fire that came not out of academic interests but out of the constant relation of his own living self to people whom he wanted to help. The result was that in a little while the other two men fell silent before him. Their voluble assertions and objections sputtered and broke like airy bubbles coming into collision with something more stable than themselves. And presently instead of protesting, they were asking questions; they were revealing the real need and emptiness for which their argumentative clatter had been only a disguise. They knew that this first man could give them something which they did not have, steadiness, assurance, certitude. They had thought that they were richer than he in information, and that, therefore, in any discussion they could be his masters; but they had found in him a fact more solid than the world of drifting ideas in which they moved, and before *that* their words rang hollow. He had the "spiritual ascendancy" of one who stood upon the sure ground of a proved experience of God.

Nor does that which such a man knows stop with himself. He helps other men first to want and then to begin to discover what he himself has found. He helps them to see in their own personalities those influences by which God becomes most intimate and convincing. A great preacher of this generation once said to a friend: "Do not look for God where He is not. Look for Him where He is." And though at first that listener was puzzled, presently she understood. What he meant was that she must stop trying to find God in abstract arguments and syllogisms; she must find Him in her own heart. And when she did, she said, "My whole idea of religion suddenly became new. He taught me to honor the little gleams of God in my own soul, to reverence whatever there was of unselfishness, of courage and of kindness there, and to know that if I believed in these enough all things were possible."

Every minister and preacher has it within his spiritual privilege to persuade men and women thus. As he goes here and there in the everyday world, and as he mingles with his people, he must look for God not where He is not but where He is. He must see God— for he can see Him—in the daily lives of ordinary folk who as yet are unaware of the dignity of their own souls because they have not dared to see that God already dwells there. He will look upon the love of mothers for their children, upon the quiet heroism of men who are bearing the burden of a difficult and uncomplaining life, upon the patience of the poor, upon the humility of some man of privilege, and he will see that in their presence he stands on holy ground. He will behold God at work in His most characteristic activity of creating men after His own image. And then in all his preaching he will help interpret these human beings to themselves. He will teach them to see the face of God reflected in their own most pure desires and in all that they love best in those who are dear to them.

He will help them feel God in all that woos them toward
their highest, so that at length they may repeat out of
their own conviction the old, true words, "We love
Him, because He first loved us." [23]

[23] I John 4:19.

CHAPTER V

HUMAN NATURE AND THE SPIRIT
OF CHRIST

T HE consideration of the Christian gospel concerning God which filled the last chapter led at its climax, as it ought to do, to an imperative for man. The great themes of religion are not developed in a vacuum. They draw into their pattern all the threads of meaning which make up human life. Obviously it makes a difference to men's opinion of themselves and of their possibilities that manhood should once have reached the sort of greatness which was reached in Jesus. Obviously it makes a difference too to believe that for men today, as for Jesus, there are available the spiritual resources of the living God. If the Christian gospel has reality in it, then the history of man is something more than anthropology. It is more than a tracing of what he has been; it is a disclosure of what he is in process of coming to be.

Or to put the matter more colloquially: What are people worth? And what are *we* worth? These are the questions to which a Christian view of life should have a particular answer.

The general opinion of our time would answer that

question with a shrug. It inclines to think that people
are worth very little even to themselves, and that in
the ultimate balance of the universe they are worth
exactly nothing at all.

There is, to begin with, a fatalistic conception of the
relation of human beings to the impersonal force of
nature. Life is regarded as only "a moment in annihilation's waste." Above the little commotion of our
human life, the cold stars look indifferently down. The
seasons come and go; another relentless winter strips
every summer of its blossoming; and the cruel ruthlessness of flood and storm and earthquake fling human lives away with no more compunction than winds
would show in scattering the petals of a dying flower.
With all his inventions and with all his fretful effort
after mastery, the powers of man are only a paper shell
against the thrust of nature when she chooses to exert
her sovereignty. The edge of an iceberg rips through
the *Titanic's* steel and sends her down to join the other
immemorial wrecks upon the ocean floor. The awful
winds of Mount Everest blow out the breath of George
Mallory and bury him in the icy drifts he dared to
defy. What is this human pilgrimage but a little trou-
bling of the dust by those whose foot-marks will presently be as though they had never been?

The description of a single scene in the experience
of a contemporary traveller may have a wider and more
cosmic reference:

"The four tents and the animated group by a well were infinitesimal specks on the desolate, limitless waste, silvered by moonlight into an unbroken sea without ripple or bourne. It was the aching solitude of nature pitted against the pathetic energy of man, and nature had no need to fight. She could leave the struggle and the stress to the human midges who would traverse her trackless silences, and when their pitiful vitality and force were spent battling with her winds and her droughts, she could bury them noiselessly in her fathomless drifts beneath the white serenity of her moons." [1]

In the second place, there is the disparagement of human personality which began with men's diminished appraisal of its origin. We may say easily today that no one is troubled any more over the doctrine of evolution; that intelligent people have accepted it and fitted it in to their whole contented picture of the truth. But that is not so. On the surface the adjustment has been brought about. People generally, including religious people, have made the thought of evolution consistent with their other thinking, and are not intellectually disturbed. But emotionally they may be disturbed more deeply than they know. There are many who have not recovered from the sub-conscious shock of thinking that human personality is only a little more elaborate

[1] I regret that I cannot find again the source of this quotation.— W. R. B.

development of the sort of life which is in the shark and the wolf and the monkey. Gamaliel Bradford wrote in his *Darwin* these sentences which describe what happened in his own spirit at the revolutionary impact of that great scientist's pronouncements: "Perhaps one may introduce oneself . . . simply as a type of a great number of average human beings, who live and suffer and have to fight their way somehow through the blinding mist of years and tears. When I was sixteen, I read the *Origin,* and I think the impression it produced has never been obliterated. . . . It is simply a feeling of utter insignificance in face of the unapprehended processes of nature, such as Leopardi expresses with bare intensity: 'Nature in all her workings has other things to think of than our good or ill.' It is a sense of being aimlessly adrift in the vast universe of consciousness, among an infinity of other atoms, all struggling desperately to assert their own existence at the expense of all the others."[2]

"And it was Darwin, the gentle, the kindly, the human, who could not bear the sight of blood, who raged against the cruelty of vivisection and slavery, who detested suffering in men or animals, it was Darwin who at least typified the rigorous logic that wrecked the universe for me and for millions of others."[3]

Nor is it only that men have been affected by their

[2] *Darwin,* by Gamaliel Bradford, p. 244. By permission of Houghton Mifflin Co.
[3] *Ibid.,* p. 247.

thought of what human life came from. They are being told that their idea that life has transcended these origins is mostly an illusion. Under the title *The Modern Temper,* one of the most influential of contemporary essayists has carried through his extraordinary tour-de-force in the deflation of human values, and in his chapter on "The Tragic Fallacy" he declares: "For us no choice remains except that between mere rhetoric and the frank consideration of our fellow men, who may be the highest of the anthropoids but who are certainly too far below the angels to imagine either that these angels can concern themselves with them or that they can catch any glimpse of even the soles of angelic feet. We can no longer tell tales of the fall of noble men because we do not believe that noble men exist. The best that we can achieve is pathos and the most that we can do is to feel sorry for ourselves." [4]

In some quarters this depreciation of human personality has become a cult. It is regarded as a mark of enlightenment to be cynical. Idealism—even moral idealism—is despised, and there is a fear of pretending to an impossible goodness which turns into a poisoned phobia against even that which is wholesomely and plainly good. For illustrations of this we do not turn to the classics. We turn rather to those impetuous expressions of opinion in which we may see contempo-

[4] *The Modern Temper. A Study and a Confession,* by Joseph Wood Krutch, p. 137.

rary impulses in the raw. They may be adolescent; they are often unpleasant; but they exist. And here, taken from the undergraduate daily newspaper of one of the great American universities, in 1934, is an editorial which shows not only how cheaply the standards of life normally held desirable can be regarded, but also how mordantly the dislike of them may be expressed. The occasion for the editorial was a letter to the President of the United States written by Charles A. Lindbergh concerning a matter of public policy with which letter the college editor happened to disagree. Whereupon he wrote:

"Apparently he expected—somewhat naïvely, one is inclined to think—that any telegram from him would simply be assumed to proceed from the most altruistic reasons. For how could the boy who flew across the ocean with only a sandwich for company, who was so blushing and modest and gawky in the face of virtual deification, who got bored at a risqué musical comedy, who ostentatiously spurned liquor and lechery, do anything ignoble? Unfortunately, Lindy has been as mistaken in his analysis of the public temper as he was in his estimation of Roosevelt's naïveté; the people are, in fact, damn sick and tired of these Clean Cut Young Men; Mr. James Cagney has been substituted as a somewhat bawdier idol, and even the self-conscious college rake with a girl on his arm, a flask on his hip, and a vacuum in his head is held to be preferable to young Master Purity. The rebuke to Lindbergh will be loudly cheered by those unfortunate men who do not look as though they worshipped Pure American Motherhood and lived the Clean Life." [5]

In the third place, the life of this time has been affected by its materialistic standards of success.

The causes which have brought this about are obvious. There never has been a period in previous human history which has made the lure of gain so great. The miracle-working progress of invention, the development of mass-production by machinery, the imperial sweep of business and commercial enterprise, enabled men to make profits on a scale never dreamed of before. The able and ambitious man could grow so rich that the fable of Midas at whose touch all things turned to gold became very nearly a picture of the actual fact. Every luxury that might be imagined, every satisfaction of the most far-flung desire, every control of a world made tributary to his tastes, seemed to be possible to the man who exploited to the full the chances the modern world gave him to make money.

Nor was it by any means only the men naturally covetous or luxury-loving who were affected by the prevalent urge for wealth. Many of the ablest men who have entered the race for money have done so not primarily because they wanted things. They wanted power. And in the civilization they were a part of,

[5] *Harvard Crimson,* March 16, 1934.

money was power. It meant control of great industrial
and financial processes. It exalted them to the seats of
the mighty.

And because it gave power, it gave also prestige. It
would be a fascinating history of western society for
the last century which should set out to trace and to
illustrate the shift in the basis of prestige. Once it was
a man's birth that gave prestige. Then it was his mem-
bership in certain traditional professions. But all this
is altered. The man who has made money has become
the man of power, and he has become also the man to
whom deference is given. He is the potential "big
giver" to whom hospitals and charitable institutions of
all sorts turn. He takes his place upon the boards of
trustees of schools and colleges. His ideas of what
may be "safe" and practical may determine large policies of education and of public affairs. And so great
had grown this gradually accepted authority of the man
of wealth that, until very recently at least, few people
insisted upon preserving the distinction between those
spheres of experience in which the rich manufacturer
or banker might really speak with knowledge, and
those other spheres with regard to which his understanding was of the crudest, but into which he was
always pushing his control. The result was that many
of the most crucial interests of the mind and spirit
were in danger of being poisoned by the subtly penetrating false idea of what constitutes success. Was not

the great captain of industry, or some arbiter of fortunes on Wall Street, obviously a successful man? Therefore let all institutions crave his leadership. The successful university would be the one which could attract the endowments of men like these. The successful church would be the one which had such distinguished persons in its pews.

It would be unfair and foolish to make exaggerated pictures of types of persons, as the cartoonists do, and then to regard all individuals in the light of these. There are and have been men eminent in those fields of activity most characteristic of the modern age, men powerful in practical affairs and builders of great fortunes, who have kept a wide and sensitive recognition of what full success should be. They have been too great to confuse the raw material of life with life itself; and they have not merely accumulated riches but have enriched the finer values of their world. Yet when this is said, the fact still stands that a conception of success which is largely mercenary has been lifted up into a contemporary idol. Because its surface glitters people have not stopped to see that its countenance is harsh and that the homage it calls for is degrading. The stories of the Old Testament often have their curiously modern duplications. It was not only in the time of Nebuchadnezzar that the commanding influence of the world has set up a golden image and ordered that all "people, nations and languages" should fall down and worship it when the music of its ritual begins to sound.

Such then are some of the aspects of the modern mood with which the Christian gospel must take account. They show what men of this time, left to themselves, are apt to be. Thus and thus actual people are thinking, feeling, choosing. What now does the Christian interpretation of life have to say to these conceptions?

. First, in regard to that fatalism into which men sometimes fall when they look at what seem to them the indifferences or the cruelties of nature. ⸰

There are, of course, religious cults which deal with these dismaying considerations of the objective world simply by withdrawing into a subjective world of amiable make-believe. They would remove unpleasant facts by incantation. "There is no pain or evil." "Every day in every way, I am growing better and better;—and so does the world, whether it knows it or not." These cheerful assertions, artificial and forced though they may seem, do have their value. They represent at any rate an affirmative and creative attitude toward the great complex of existence. But their weakness is that they over-simplify. They pretend to deal with life when what they are doing is to deal with only that part which fits into their formula, and to ignore the inconvenient remainder. But a full Christian gospel cannot so cavalierly ride around the facts. It must have in it not only a courageous optimism but a steady realism as well. It will recognize that the world we live in does have its baffling contradictions. It is not easy to set men at rest with phrases when they are confronted by those relentless processes of nature which seem to have so little concern for human life. How shall they believe in a God of love when they see what appears to be the cynical impartiality of flood one year and drought the next; when they contemplate typhoid fever and infantile paralysis; and when they ponder the ultimate fate of life itself here on this cooling planet where humanity leads its lonely and foredoomed existence in the midst of the uninhabited and indifferent stars?

The first element of the answer which the Christian gospel gives to this first contradiction is its invincible belief, shaped by the impact of existence as a whole upon the consciousness, that human life and the human spirit do matter—and that the universe is geared to their production, not to their extermination. That belief obviously involves an act of faith. It must maintain itself in the face of partial facts that bring denial. But the point is that in this crucial matter faith is less difficult, and more reasonable, than unfaith. For here is the inescapable and evident fact that the universe did produce man as the flower of its long evolution. In his mind alone does the question wake as to whether the universe has meaning, and what the meaning is. Physically he may seem insignificant as measured against

the bulk of all other created things. But if there is any
sense in creation at all, it is he that reflects and focuses
that sense. The human being may be only a moving
atom in comparison with the immensity of the stars;
but if it be asked how man dares to take himself seriously in face of the infinities which astronomy reveals,
the answer—in the clear words of another—is that
man is the astronomer; and if there is majesty in the
heavens or on the earth, it is he that has found it out.

It is certain that Jesus had this sense of the transcendent worth of man. He did not put it in phrases
such as that. He did not argue; but he built all that he
saw and did upon a deep assumption. The created universe is friendly to human beings. Notwithstanding all
the terrible things that cut across it, the road which
mankind walks upon is a road of increasing life. When
men act upon this faith, they go from strength to
strength.

Let it be remembered that this faith which is at the
heart of the Christian gospel is no sudden flurry of
assertion. It has not been born in a vacuum. It is an
expression of the invincible instinct which human consciousness at its highest has continually asserted not
with its face turned away from facts, but with its eyes
wide open to the most stubborn facts which life presented. Evil and pain and disease and disaster are no
new things which men of today must for the first time
reckon with. They have been in the world always. The

religion of the Old Testament, and the faith of Jesus, never made light of reality. They took account of the callousness of circumstances and the brutality of men. They had their victims upon whom "the tower of Siloam fell," and their "Galileans whose blood Pilate mingled with their sacrifices." Neither the psalmists nor the prophets nor Jesus ever hinted that evil did not exist. They knew it did. But the extraordinary thing has been that, recognizing evil and in spite of it they went on to believe in, and to live by, the love of God that burned through every contradiction. They dared to say, "The Lord shall preserve thee from all evil," [6] and "I thank thee, O Father, Lord of heaven and earth!" [7]

Now it is not possible to prove abstractly that the human spirit is stronger than the impersonal forces of the world. It is not possible to answer *why* evil, *why* disaster, and the rest. Nor is it possible to see in advance how God will prevail against the elements that seem intractable to His purpose. But this is what the practical boldness of religion does achieve: it makes men and women feel that when they are living at their fullest—or in other words letting their minds, their sympathies, and their strength be obedient to the highest leadings they can know—that then they do obviously push back the frontiers of evil and widen the ground over which the good life has control. They bring light where there used to be ignorance, health

[6] Psalm 121:7.　　　　[7] Matthew 11:25.

179

where there used to be disease, good will where there used to be confusion. They plant ideals in the minds of children, as the inspired teacher does; they stamp out plagues, as the pioneer of medicine does; they lead the life of nations a little farther from the old jungles of savagery and hate, as the consecrated statesman does. And when they do this, though they may have as much difficulty as ever in explaining why the human spirit is more powerful than the harsh fate which is all that the materialists believe in, they feel that it is; and in all their best work they are inwardly sure that they are not alone, but that they are fellow-workers with God.

When this is said, candor requires the immediate recognition of a contrary fact. Some ecclesiastics, more bent upon rhetorical assurances than upon reality, are fond of saying that there is no longer any conflict between religion and science. Whatever this phrase may mean, it is certain that there is conflict between what is generally supposed to be religion and the views of many scientists. A recent statistical study by James H. Leuba, professor of psychology in Bryn Mawr College, has been published under the title of "Religious Beliefs of American Scientists." [8] Following a similar inquiry made in 1914, he wrote in 1933 to a representative number of the leading American scientists and

---

[8] *Harpers Magazine*, August, 1934. By permission of Professor James H. Leuba, and Harper & Brothers.

asked them to mark for acceptance or rejection these statements: "(A) I believe in a God to whom one may pray in the expectation of receiving an answer. By 'answer' I mean more than the natural, subjective, psychological effect of prayer. (B) I do not believe in a God as defined above. (C) I have no definite belief regarding this question."

Concerning the form of the statement and the questions involved, Professor Leuba goes on to comment as follows: "I chose to define God as given above because that is the God worshipped in every branch of the Christian religion. In the absence of a belief in a God who hears and sympathises with man, and who, under certain conditions, answers his prayers, traditional worship could not go on. It appeared to me, therefore, of the greatest interest to secure definite information regarding the prevalence of that belief among scientists and students."

The resulting essay sums up in statistical forms the answers, together with quotations from the replies of certain individuals among those who answered. Professor Leuba groups his replies under four heads: those respectively from physicists, biologists, sociologists, and psychologists.

Then Professor Leuba adds: "If class distinctions are disregarded and all the scientists put together, one gets 30 per cent of believers in a God moved to action by the traditional Christian worship: supplication, thanksgiving, songs of praise, etc; 56 per cent of disbelievers; and 14 per cent of doubters."

THE BELIEF IN GOD[9]

	BELIEVERS	DIS-BELIEVERS	DOUBTERS
Physicists........	38	47	16
Biologists........	27	60	13
Sociologists.......	24	67	9
Psychologists.....	10	79	12

"The order in which the four classes of scientists place themselves with regard to the proportion of believers should by no means be disregarded. The scientists concerned with inanimate matter come first with the largest percentage (38 per cent), and those concerned with the mind come last (10 per cent); the biologists and the sociologists occupy intermediate positions. Does a knowledge of animal and plant life make belief in an interventional God difficult, while psychological learning makes it almost impossible?"

In his final summary of these and other figures Professor Leuba thus concludes: "The statistics presented in the preceding pages have revealed that the larger proportions of believers are found in the following categories of persons: (1) the scientists who know

[9] These figures represent percentages, and as Professor Leuba writes in a footnote: "The total of the believers, disbelievers, and doubters in any group should be 100; but as I counted as one the halves and the fractions over the half and dropped the other fractions, the sum may be 101 or 99."

least about living matter, society, and the mind;
(2) the less eminent men in every branch of science;
(3) the scientists and students of twenty years ago;
(4) the students in the lower college classes."

In other words to put the matter with a bluntness
from which he himself refrains, Professor Leuba's
conclusion is that the more of science any one knows
the less apt he is to believe in God; and that religious
belief runs parallel with ignorance and immaturity.

This conclusion will doubtless have been widely read,
and also widely assented to. Many who were dis-
inclined toward religion already will feel much fortified in their disinclination. "It is what we always supposed," they will say. "Now religion is ruled out among
men who matter."

But religion has been thus academically done to
death more than once before; and as stubbornly as
Banquo's ghost, and more substantially, it comes alive
again. So also it will do in spite of the thrust of Professor Leuba's statistics. And some of the reasons why
are these:

In the first place, the definition of God under which
the scientists are asked to register their belief or disbelief is a confusing one. The question on its surface
sounds fair enough. Do you believe "in a God to
whom one may pray in the expectation of receiving an
answer?" But the slant which this question carries in
Professor Leuba's mind, and presumably may have

carried therefore in the minds of many to whom he addressed it, is shown by some of his further incidental and unstudied phrases. He is thinking of "a God moved to action by the traditional Christian worship: supplication, thanksgiving, songs of praise, etc."; in brief, "an interventional God."

Now it is quite true that it has been "an interventional God" who has been worshipped in much of the "traditional" practice of the churches; and it is true that traditional theology has often thought of God as an external power to be "moved to action . . . by supplication, thanksgiving, songs of praise, etc."; but it is not this conception of God that the more thoughtful and the more experienced hold. God is not, as certain Christian teachers, a little wearied by all the bland misconceptions, have pointed out, "a cosmic bell-hop," whose existence is to be proved only as He comes running from somewhere to answer our demands. He is the Spirit of Life moving through all life. He is the great Companion, whom our spirits know when they begin to deal with life on those ranges which take all that a man has, and more; and therefore force us, at the end of our own resources, to desire, and then to become aware of, a Spirit that fulfils our own. It is not by waiting to see whether an "interventional" something projects itself into our external world that we find God. He is not to be watched for, as men watch for a strange comet; He is to be experienced, as men

experience the energy streaming from the sun. Nor is
it by "supplication, thanksgiving, songs of praise, etc."
that he is to "be moved to action." He is in action
already, wherever life is growing toward its best; and
those who try to ally themselves with His purpose as
this becomes revealed to the sensitiveness of an inner
worship, will find their public worship simply an instinctive dramatization of what they already know.
Their conviction of God is based not on derivative
arguments from certain aspects of the world which
their intellects have contemplated; it is based upon an
assurance they have received in the process of courageous living. They cannot prove that the God whom
they thus experience is one with whom the whole great
universe of suns and stars and flowers and living
things will be seen to be in tune. Here they frankly
make the venture of faith; but the fact is that this faith
gives an increase of effective energy to life itself, and
on the ground of its results can rest its truth.

A second reason why statistics on "Religious Beliefs
of American Scientists" do not necessarily control the
destinies of religion is that it is only naïveté which
assumes that scientists are authorities in this matter.
As we have already suggested in another connection,
there is a curious tendency in our American mind to
give a kind of gaping hero-worship to any individual
or group which arouses its astonishment—like ado-
lescents who being fascinated by some one who knows

a great deal about something are sure that he must
know everything. Our contemporaries have gazed with
awe upon the big business man; and although the great
scientist is a very different sort of man, nevertheless he
has been accorded the same sort of uncritical awe, and
partly because of the same reason. For the scientist
through his discoveries has originally made possible,
and directly or indirectly furnishes now, many of the
things to which modern men attach most value. How
should we have had our railroads and steamships, our
telephones and electric light and automobiles and airplanes and radios, without the scientists? All sorts of
miracles seem to come out of laboratories. Why then
should not the miracle workers know everything about
the world, and about a God who did or did not make it?

So men ask; and they think the answer is self-evi-
dent. But as a matter of fact, the answer is quite different from what the hasty popular notion would have
it. A scientist as such is not necessarily an authority
on anything outside his special science. "Many of us
are inclined to call a man wise if he understands things
like the Bohr atom and the Einstein theory. That, too,
is a mistake. He is not really wise; he is only intelligent." [10]

Unless in addition to his science, the scientist is a
man who is creatively at grips with life, his science
may make him less rather than more qualified to esti-

[10] *A Primer for Tomorrow,* by Christian Gauss, p. 117.

mate religious truth. For as a scientist he is dealing
with things which are being taken apart; and religion
belongs rather in the process by which things are put
together. He is dealing with weights and measurements, with quantities and classifications, with the what
of things rather than with the why. He is bent upon
scrutinizing the elements out of which his particular
part of the universe is made up; he may not be culti-
vating the ability to see the larger relationships which
give these their ultimate meaning. Nobody would consider it especially appropriate that a group of scientists,
graded according to their scientific eminence, should on
that account be enlisted as a jury to determine the
beauty of a particular symphony. Watches keep time,
and watchmakers mend watches; but nobody would se-
lect a group of watchmakers to make final pronounce-
ment upon the nature of time and upon how to make
the best use of it. Life functions in a human body, and
the anatomist searches that body for its physical secrets;
but this is not to say that the anatomist will know most
about the meaning of life. So it may not be the scientist who will prove most qualified to say whether the
infinite Life which man believes he touches in the universe is or is not there. By the very nature of what He
is believed to be, God cannot make Himself most surely
known to specialists. Rather must He reveal Himself
most surely to those, whether intrinsically learned or
unlearned, who meet life on the widest front. The faith

by which the whole personality can be mastered, even
when the intellect alone might hesitate, has seldom been
more nobly expressed than by this passage from the
autobiography of Albert Schweitzer, one of those
many-sided geniuses whom the world only occasionally
brings forth, great musician, theologian, physician, and
servant of human kind. Against the background of his
hospital in equatorial Africa, and against all the tragic
human needs to which he had deliberately given his life,
he wrote: "To the question whether I am a pessimist
or an optimist, I answer that my knowledge is pessimistic, but my willing and hoping are optimistic. . . .
However much concerned I was at the problem of the
misery in the world, I never let myself get lost in
broodings over it; I always held firmly to the thought
that each one of us can do a little to bring some portion
of it to an end. Thus I came gradually to rest content
in the knowledge that there is only one thing we can
understand about the problem, and that is that each
of us has to go his own way, but as one who means to
help to bring about deliverance. . . . Because I have
confidence in the power of truth and of the spirit, I
believe in the future of mankind." [11]

And with his words may be listed those of another
gallant wrestler with life and creator of goodness for
his fellowmen, Sir Wilfred Grenfell: "In view of the

[11] *Out of My Life and Thought*, pp. 279, 280, 281. By permission
of George Allen & Unwin Ltd., London, and Henry Holt and Company.

eight years I spent among the purlieus of Whitechapel, the garrets and common lodging-houses around the East India docks, and, since, among the debt-ridden and often half-starved poor of these northern shores, I can understand how pessimists come into existence." . . . But this "is what life means to me. It means a chance for every one to be helping lame dogs over stiles, a chance to be cheering and helping to bear the burdens of others, a field for the translation of unfailing faith in the love of God above into deeds that shall please his children below, and therefore please him also. . . . Life to me is ever beautiful. Life is a thousand times worth while." [12]

There is another question concerning man and his relationship to the forces of his universe which is linked with the question of his belief in God. That is the question of immortality. When Professor Leuba wrote to his American scientists to ask whether they believed in a God to whom one may pray in the expectation of receiving an answer, he also asked them whether they believed in survival after death. "The proportion of believers," he reports, "is nearly equal: 33 per cent for immortality and 30 per cent for God." It sounds like a bulletin of an election in which Professor Leuba assumes that God is a candidate, and by returns from which he is prepared to count Him out of office. "But," he continues, "there is a much smaller

[12] *What Life Means to Me,* pp. 5, 13, 6.

number of downright disbelievers in immortality: forty-
one per cent against fifty-six per cent."

The soul of man, then, leads God in the balloting for
survival. But even so it loses the election. With reference to both, extinction wins.

So much for the verdict of Professor Leuba's figures. They are entitled to respect, and they will receive
it. It is important to know what men of science think,
for are they not, as Professor Leuba says, "men whose
task is the discovery and teaching of the truth regarding the universe and man"?

As a matter of fact, no. They are not in the main
discoverers and teachers of "the truth." They are discoverers and teachers of many *truths,* in the sense of
many particular facts about the world and men. But the
characteristic activities of the scientist are predominantly, and sometimes narrowly, intellectual—not emotional nor volitional. His awareness of reality is
through one part of a man's full nature, not through all;
and the danger immediately arises that part of reality
may therefore be beyond the range of his concentrated
scrutiny. There are things he does not believe in about
life, but his disbelief here does not invalidate the belief
of others; because the sphere in which he is an authority is the laboratory, not life. Therefore it is possible that men and women technically less learned than
he may through their deep knowledge of the human
soul in its actual dreams, its hopes, its loves, its suffer-

ings, and its triumphs, have a surer intuition about that soul's destiny than the scientific specialist can ever deduce from the segregated facts he knows.

To deal adequately with the Christian faith in immortality would require a volume in itself. The expression of men's thinking about it is one of the massive and majestic elements in the long record of human thought. Generation after generation, men have been confronted with what seemed the stark disaster of death; but invincibly they have gone on believing that the growing richness which the spirit gathers to itself in this life is not meant to be scattered, but goes on into larger employment in a life to come. Like belief in God, it is not a demonstration, but a faith that kindles into fire through a life lived daringly. It develops not like a syllogism, but like the sweep of a symphony, completing a theme that was born not of argument but of inspiration—inspiration which, as always, seems to come not from a man's own mind but from ineffable realities that break through the envelope of his little life.

Nor is it only to the greatly endowed that this conviction of immortal life may come. Here again the old words may be true: "Where is the wise? where is the scribe? where is the disputer of this world? . . . God hath chosen the foolish things of the world to confound the wise." [13] Men and women of every rank, who

[13] I Corinthians 1:20, 27.

are learning to live religiously, and who thereby experience God and see life illumined by the fact of God, have an assurance of immortality such as no evidence of test-tubes or telescopes can give or take away. "We may stress the fact that calm, untroubled assurance comes through the religious relation with God. There is, I think, no human knowledge so certain as that which comes of close acquaintance with a personality whose character is well-developed. Formed personality is the most flexible of all things in its action but the most stable in its attitudes. The stone which has served me for a foothold going up the mountain may drop on my head on the way down. But I know that the trustworthy guide who helped me up will help me in any emergencies that arise in the descent. I can offer no scientific evidence that my wife will tend me when I am ill or that my mother will help me out of a scrape, yet on occasion I may know these things with a finality that belongs to no other sort of fact. The airy clouds of what we used to call the solid physical universe may swirl into this form or that at the bidding of Einstein, Eddington, and Jeans, but through these cosmic storms the great personalities pursue a serene, determinate way. There is no rock so solid on which to found one's life as the character of a splendid personality. So out of the religious knowledge of acquaintance with God as distinguished from knowledge about God comes the power to say with complete certainty, 'He will not let me, in whom the will to live runs strong, forever die.' " [14]

Those last sentences are a quotation, and as such they have a singular validity. For they were written by a man who not only in his words but in his daily work, and not only in his living but in his dying, bore witness to the power which can come through faith in life immortal. They are taken from a little book by Wilbur Cosby Bell, professor at the Theological Seminary in Virginia, published after his death in the prime of a happy and abundant life. Stricken with abrupt unexpectedness by a heart attack, and told by the doctors that he had only a few more hours on this earth, he took that news with a glow of new expectancy. For several hours, oblivious to pain, he talked with his wife of their life that had been together, and of the life he believed was opening ahead. And then he dictated to her this message to the men he taught:

"Tell the boys that I've grown surer of God every year of my life, and I've never been so sure as I am right now. . . . I'm so glad to find that I haven't the least shadow of shrinking or uncertainty. . . . I've always thought so and now that I'm right up against it, I know." Again he went on: "Life owes me nothing. I've had work I loved, and I've lived in a beautiful place among congenial friends. I've had love in its highest form and I've got it forever. . . . I can see now that death is just the smallest thing—just an accident

[14] *If a Man Die*, by W. Cosby Bell, pp. 30-31.

—that it means nothing. There's no real break—God is there—and life—and all that really counts in life—goes on." [15]

We pass on now to consider the bearing of the Christian gospel upon the second of the tendencies already noted in the present-day estimate of what humanity amounts to. There was, in the first place, as we have seen, a pessimism in the face of what seems the indifference or relentlessness of nature. And, second, there is the depreciation of human personality in a world where moral standards are adrift in a welter of change.

It is true that we have not yet quite adjusted ourselves to the shock which came to human self-esteem when the doctrine of evolution was first proclaimed. Intellectually we have become reconciled to it; but in obscure emotional attitudes many people are still feeling its sub-conscious dislocation. It is easier to be complacent about a past than to build a future; and many people, when their ideas of aristocratic racial pedigree seemed suddenly to be riddled, fall victims to the suggestion that since their origins seemed bestial, therefore they are bestial, and might as well remain so. It requires a largeness of thought and a boldness of spirit which some people shrink from in order to see that the process of creation becomes not the less but the more noble and inspiring when it is seen as not a sudden

[15] *Ibid.*, p. 199.

fiat of God that made man complete, but the steady working of the divine spirit with which man can himself co-operate, toward an end which is not yet complete.

In every age the first requisite for great living is that men should believe thus in the essential divineness of their growing souls; but in the present time, more than in most periods of history, that belief must be fought for against serious denial. We have all round us a chorus of voices crying out with every kind of smart and satiric accent that there is no divineness in man at all, but only beastliness. We originated in a common ancestry with the brutes—they say—and essential brutes we are and will remain. There is a fountain of that kind of belief, flowing like dirty water, through much of our modern literature and some of our most popular magazines. There is a cult of depreciation, and before its degraded idol many who think themselves in the mode of present-day smartness must bow down.

A rabbi, Abba Hillel Silver, in a book which he calls *Religion in a Changing World,* has cogently expressed the contrast between some of our contemporary thinking and the message which all high religion must seek to bring:

"This new life is, after all, no new life at all, but an acceleration of the old rhythm—a swifter scansion of an hackneyed melody. The irreverences and the irresponsibilities of our day are no whit different from the stale bravadoes of every generation since the beginning of time—the same capers and the same totems. There is nothing new in novelty! . . .

"The New Life is not a new excitement, but a new exultation—not a stimulant, but a satisfaction. We renew ourselves, not by indulging our appetites, but by improving our tastes. We enter new worlds through the gates of aspiration.

"Religion has long known this. It therefore refuses to be impressed by the heathen ragings of our day. Its wisdom is the cumulative wisdom of the ages. Its moral theses have been tested by time and are grounded in the millennial experiences of the race. It is not an amateur in the matter of human relations. It has lived intimately with man through vast cycles of time and it has learned to understand him critically, to judge him sympathetically and to guide him steadfastly along the narrow way of self-discipline. In a world of shifting standards, of moral drift and confusion, religion proclaims today, as of yore, its few simple, strong, unalterable convictions touching the basic sanctities of human life." [16]

There was another voice, this time a Christian one, who also had something to say about the "simple, strong, unalterable convictions touching the basic sanctities of human life." Frederick W. Robertson, greatest of English-speaking preachers and interpreters of the spirit of Christ, wrote in his journal at an hour of

[16] *Religion in a Changing World,* by Abba Hillel Silver, pp. 161, 180. By permission of Harper & Brothers.

personal inner crisis: "It is an awful moment when the soul begins to find that the props on which it has blindly rested so long are, many of them, rotten, and begins to suspect them all; when it begins to feel the nothingness of many of the traditionary opinions which have been received with implicit confidence, and in that horrible insecurity begins also to doubt whether there be anything to believe at all. It is an awful hour—let him who has passed through it say how awful—when this life has lost its meaning, and seems shrivelled into a span; when the grave appears to be the end of all, human goodness nothing but a name, and the sky above this universe a dead expanse, black with the void from which God Himself has disappeared. In that fearful loneliness of spirit, when those who should have been his friends and counsellors only frown upon his misgivings, and profanely bid him stifle doubts which, for aught he knows, may arise from the fountain of truth itself; to extinguish, as a glare from hell, that which, for aught he knows, may be light from heaven, and every thing seems wrapped in hideous uncertainty, I know but one way in which a man may come forth from his agony scatheless; it is by holding fast to those things which are certain still—the grand, simple landmarks of morality. In the darkest hour through which a human soul can pass, whatever else is doubtful, this at least is certain. If there be no God and no future state yet even then it is better to be generous than selfish, better to be chaste than licentious, better to be true than false, better to be brave than to be a coward. Blessed beyond all earthly blessedness is the man who, in the tempestuous darkness of the soul, has dared to hold fast to these venerable landmarks. Thrice blessed is he who—when all is drear and cheerless within and without, when his teachers terrify him, and his friends shrink from him—has obstinately clung to moral good. Thrice blessed, because *his* night shall pass into clear, bright day.

"I appeal to the recollection of any man who has passed through that hour of agony, and stood upon the rock at last, the surges stilled below him, and the last cloud drifted from the sky above, with a faith, and hope, and trust no longer traditional, but of his own— a trust which neither earth nor hell shall shake thenceforth forever." [17]

But *why* is all this true, and how shall a man believe it? Many people today are adrift with no such anchors as these which Robertson could let down. Their ideas about elemental morality are questions, not convictions. There is no decisiveness in their sense of right and wrong. "Better to be true than false, pure than impure"—how do they know? And if they did know, what can they do about it? Do not the behaviorists teach that personality is nothing but reaction to outward stimulus; and do not the Freudians say that all

[17] *Life and Letters of Frederick W. Robertson*, edited by Stopford A. Brooke, p. 86.

behavior can be traced back to one primitive instinct which men share with all the rest of the animal creation? If we are pushed this way and that by physical and instinctive forces, why talk about moral responsibility? Things will be as they will be, and in the long run there is not much difference between one thing and another.

From that sort of bewilderment of values, with the consequent disintegration of personality, what can save? Not arguments. Rather, the evidence of a fact. In this realm of questioning, men must *see* in order to believe. Clever manipulations of words can entangle them in a net of sophistries. But when some supreme personality moves across the horizon of their life, he walks through the web and the sophistries snap like thread before him. The doubts and denials of even the plainest ethical realities which look so plausible on the pages of a clever book shrivel before the impact of one convincing life.

And it is here that the Christian gospel brings its incomparable gift. For it does not weave an argument. It does not offer a code. It brings instead a great Figure. It says, "Look at him. See in him the creative power of personality made so evident that you cannot doubt it. Recognize in him those elements of character which once you have seen them you know to be supreme."

Jesus of Nazareth was born in an obscure province

which meant little to the masters of his world. He grew up in an unregarded town. Most of his life was lived among peasants in Galilee; and after a few months of public activity, during which the great ones of his country grew increasingly hostile and only "the common people heard him gladly," [18] he died upon a cross. Yet from that brief moment of time, and from those circumstances which seemed made up only of obscurity or of disaster, the personality of Jesus has emerged with a power which dominates the imagination of the centuries. The significance of Augustus Cæsar and Tiberius is as dead as their long-buried dust. Names like those of Herod and of Pilate, and of other figures whose shadows lay large across their time, are saved from oblivion only because they had to do with Jesus. But he who possessed none of the things they possessed, he whose greatness was only in his soul, exerts his unending fascination still upon the minds and hearts and wills of men. If we seek for "self-expression," it is there. If we want to know whether a life can master circumstances, we look at him and know.

And the further fact about Jesus is that his personality never seems to stand alone. He does not make others feel their littleness because he was so great. He wakes, instead, a wondering sense of potential greatness in all the souls who are drawn toward him. A recent visitor to India wrote of Mahatma Gandhi: "In

[18] Mark 12:37.

his presence I felt a new capability and power in myself rather than a consciousness of his power. I felt
equal, confident, good for anything—an assurance I
had never known before, as if some consciousness
within me had newly awakened. A man who can do this
to people can mould his age." *Jesus* did that to people,
and in consequence he moulded not only some men in
his own age, but through them gradually he moulded
the ages.

The influence of Jesus upon his first disciples was
like sunlight on a planted seed. Slumbering aspirations
in them began to quiver. Hidden possibilities in them
began to wake. This man, this strong and confident
Jesus, believed in them. He thought of them not as
fishermen and peasants, not as the ordinary and humdrum characters which they had always been. He
thought of them as sons of God, meant to attain divine
fulfilment. So they began to move in the direction of
Jesus' belief, Simon Peter, James, John, and Andrew
and the rest. And they went so far in the way of
growth which he inspired that they have left their mark
on history.

If it were asked that the effect of Jesus upon human
personalities should be summed up in a sentence, the
answer might be this : that he gives men a joyous sense
of how great life can be, and that he brings them into
judgment concerning the limitations that hold them
back.

We need to capture this first impression at the very outset if we would understand the genius of Christianity. Jesus has been called the Man of Sorrows, and there is truth in that, for his great nature sounded the deeps of human experience. But in an even vaster sense, he was the man of joy. He loved the fair beauty of this earth, and he found it good and saw it full of God. Mark how the beauty of it flashes again and again through his speech in figure and in parable. Reading the Gospels, one can hear him thinking aloud, thinking of nesting birds, of spring days when the sower goes through the fields to scatter seed in the ground, of the strange miracle of that seed growing under the starlight and under the warmth of the noonday sun, of sunrises and sunsets and the changing signs of the weather, of shepherd and sheep and tinkling bells, and the gathering of lambs into the folds at night. He watched the careless flight of sparrows. He said to his disciples, God will take care of you as He takes care of them. He saw the lilies growing in the wheat, and he told his disciples that they also could grow into beauty if their roots went down to God. He helped them to find their whole world sacramental because it was full of the poetry by which the commonest things could suggest the wonder of God.

Men live today under conditions which make them often conscious not of the beauty of the world, but of its ugliness, not of its hope but of its heaviness, not of its life but of its load. We know about disease germs, and accidents, and epidemics and death. We know about the drive of drab duties, work that grows to be a hateful routine, life that walks up and down in its grooves of brick, until we in our modern civilization seem sometimes as prisoners in a cell. So it may come about that we are like men under a leaden sky, playing the game of life with dice which seem loaded with dreariness if not with defeat. But as we look into our deeper consciousness, we can remember other and different experiences. Rare is the man who cannot remember certain impressions of his boyhood which are as fresh now as dew upon the morning fields, of days when he woke with the sheer joy of living because the spring sunshine was pouring in the window and he had no more responsibilities than a colt let loose, of the stir of leaves in old trees when the morning breeze blew from the sunrise, of the smell of woods and of dew-wet leaves on the silent ground, of dappled sunlight on the river where he went to swim. And have there not been hours also in the maturer years, hours which can forever be repeated, when the freshness of the boy spirit and all the thrilling openness of the world come flooding back? Stand on the mountain-top at dawn and see the opalescent sunrise quivering through the clouds; walk on the sands by moonlight where the white-maned squadrons of the sea come thundering toward the shore when the wind blows in from the horizon; stand by some still lake in the woods and look up to the winter or the summer stars;—and into the soul there floods the consciousness that the world is good and that life is unspeakably worth living.

That is the impression which Jesus brought to his disciples, not in momentary flashes only but as a continually repeated consciousness. Bigger than all the contradictions of evil or of pain, bigger than all the little doubts and discouragements, was the great, englobing fact of the beauty of God. If they had stopped to analyze it all, the disciples perhaps would sometimes have lost the joy they had. But under the spell of Jesus' personality, they knew that this joy was theirs, and that it was real. The same experience has flowered through the Christian centuries, like bulbs bringing again and again their fragrance in recurring springs. Saint Francis of Assisi knew it. The old hymn-writer who wrote "Fairest Lord Jesus, Ruler of all nature," knew it. Other men and women, in their various times and ways, have known it. When men say, "I believe in Jesus Christ," they are believing in him who moved through his world with the sunlight in his eyes, with the thrill and splendor as of dawn around him, with the quiver of spirit which communicates itself to their own spirits and makes them feel deep down in their souls that truth is not in the darkness but in the touch of the expanding day.

Such then was, and is, the first way in which Jesus

affects the personalities of men. He makes them feel the urge of life, by showing them how great it ought to be. And then—as we have said—he brings them into judgment. There is no mistaking the fact that his presence among people resulted in drastic distinctions. "I am come," he said, "not to send peace but a sword." [19] The thrust of his ideas divided men inevitably; on the one hand, those whose souls leaped to admire him and to follow him; and those, on the other hand, whose consciences felt the disturbance of his influence but who hated him for the unrest he provoked in them.

Sometimes men judged themselves in Jesus' presence. The influence of his personality was automatic in them. They gave their own verdict upon themselves either by the fact of rallying to him or by the fact of recoiling into the ring of his enemies. By their own motion they were ranged among those who stood on his right hand or on his left. But sometimes also Jesus himself gave voice to the judgments which were taking place, and it is significant to see when and against whom his judgments were levelled.

The men whom he judged most sternly were the ones who might ordinarily have expected to be judged least. They were particularly the leaders of his church. The Pharisees themselves were full of denunciations for the orthodox kind of sins. They despised the common people who were not pious. They were shocked at all the

[19] Matthew 10:34.

obvious delinquencies. When they found a woman who
had sinned, their moral ferocity wanted to satisfy itself by stoning her. Against all the ordinary lapses of
the flesh, they set their faces of judgment hard as flint,
and it never occurred to them that they themselves were
in danger of judgment. Yet it was against these and
not against the common people, not against the Zac-
cheuses and the women who had sinned, that Jesus
flashed the lightnings of his withering condemnation.
In the twenty-third chapter of the Gospel according to
Saint Matthew are written words which to this day blis-
ter and burn. He judged the leaders of the church because they had had every opportunity to know and love
the real goodness of God, and yet had blinded themselves to the very meaning which goodness ought to
have. They could condemn others, but they would not
even examine themselves. They took pride in their
frozen morality, but all the while they were full of intolerance, and merciless self-righteousness. They not
only would not go into the kingdom of heaven themselves, but by the very fact of what they were they kept
others out. It is as though he said,—and says: "to
think that you are righteous because you have never
been misled by physical passion, to think that you are
holy because you are pharisaical, to be too fearful of
the mob opinion of the pious to listen compassionately
to the truth, to make zeal for the moral law a synonym
for intolerance and exaggeration and vindictive bitter-

ness,—this is to poison at its very source the distinction between good and evil and to destroy that sensitiveness of the soul which is its life."

Let us be quite clear about this. Jesus was no indulgent sentimentalist. He did not overlook the sin of the perverted will or the sin of evil impulses weakly yielded to anywhere or in any person. He saw these always for the marring of the image of God in man which they are. Nobody ever got from him the idea that moral distinctions did not matter. When he saved the woman in the temple from the implacable Pharisees, he said to her, "Go, and sin no more." [20] When his tenderness stooped to pity the woman in Simon the Pharisee's house it was in order that he might lift her up to be a saint. No one ever found in him an excuse for continuing in the paths of any evil. Those who were nearest and dearest to him knew as well as any did the inflexible insistence of a love that was inspiring because it would not let them drop lower than their best. "Get thee behind me, Satan," [21] he said once to the awestruck Peter when Peter's mood of cowardice and self-saving tried to tempt his Master to take the easier way for himself and for the disciples. The look in those eyes of his, so clear, so steady, and so deep, was a judgment which could not be escaped.

So that character of Jesus judged men in the ancient time. So equally it judges now. The glib voices of the

[20] John 8:11.   [21] Mark 8:33.

world which like to call themselves new proclaim that old ideas of morality are obsolete. Why should you not follow the impulses of the flesh, they say, and be free in self-expression? Why be inhibited by antique notions of purity and chastity and all other such names that belong to the pale atmosphere of monasteries and nunneries, and not to the red blood of the real world? Why not listen to the modern voices and go free? And then within the natural clean-mindedness of the thoughtful boy or girl something else arises. A figure is there, virile and strong and beautiful. It is the figure of Jesus. And they hear his voice: "This so-called freedom that seeks to lure you is only a freedom to be an animal. It would mean not freedom, but only slavery for you who are made to be a child of God. You cannot win distinction by way of commonness. You cannot gain the glory of your human life by being sub-human. These new ideas which you are tempted to wear as a badge of distinction—look at them closer and see whether they are not merely the leprosy of unclean desire and subverted will, from which you need to be cleansed." And out of a deep response, the finest of our young people will make their genuine answer, the answer of allegiance, not to the Jesus who is a far-off figure in history, but to that Jesus who is implicitly the Christ in them.

Men can review their lives in other aspects also than those which have to do with moral temptation. They may ask themselves what contribution they may be making to the times in which they live. If they answer that question by standards which are non-Christian, they may perhaps find easy ground for complacency. "Am I not a thoroughly respectable citizen?" one says. "Have I not builded a family and maintained it in comfort? Men count me successful in my business or my profession." So far, so good. Before the casual jury of the world's opinion such a man may go free to cultivate his own self-praise; but there is a loftier judgment, and it is a judgment which he cannot evade, because he carries it always within himself. No matter how men may think they have got rid of it, that judgment of Jesus which has to do with realities is always there. They may tell themselves, "I do not believe in him any more." They may be obsessed with all sorts of glib arguments against what they call his divinity. They may say that they do not hold with the creeds, have no use for the church, are not by confession even Christians. Nevertheless, they cannot get away from the spirit of Jesus. He has entered into the warp and woof of the ideals of our civilization, those ideals whose force and expectancy we cannot fail to know. And so even when men or women are most prone to be content with selfish achievements, something tall and beautiful rises up in their soul to ask them, "What high loyalty are you following? What have you done to show that a great life comes not to be ministered unto but to minister? What have you done to put into fact what you know you recognize, that he that is greatest is he that doth serve?"

So within us in a hundred ways that figure of Jesus rises. So continually his eyes look upon us, his voice speaks to us, his finger points unerringly at the realities which we try to gloss over with specious names. He reveals to us our own recognition because he is not something other than our own souls, but the expression of the truest—even though hitherto the unguessed—instinct in ourselves.

Moreover, it is true that this subjection to the judgment of Jesus is the only thing that makes men really free. Who are the free people in this world? And who are the slaves? The slaves are the people who acknowledge no great mastership. They have never submitted themselves to any single loyalty so great, so beautiful, and so compelling that their whole soul rises up spontaneously to follow it. The result is that, having no direction of their own, they are blown about by every vagrant wind of influence. They will listen to any voice, wear the label of any cheap but popular idea, copy any fashion. People run in crowds, think in crowds, feel in crowds. They are afraid to discriminate, or to express discrimination if they have it. They think they are free because there is nothing to which inwardly they have bound themselves to be loyal. But the end is that they have no more freedom than an empty boat which follows the eddies of a flowing river.

But what does make a free man? The greatest and most glorious of all the servants of Jesus knew. Paul the Apostle gloried in being what he called the "bond-servant" of Jesus Christ. No words were too strong to express his sense of glad surrender to him who was his Lord. "Nevertheless I live," he said, "yet not I, but Christ liveth in me." [22] He had a master; yes. And, as he wrote to the Romans, when a man has a master, "to his own master he standeth or falleth"; and, as he wrote to the Galatians, "Let no *man* trouble me." [23] That was the result of his willing and spontaneous subjection to the authority of Jesus dwelling in his own soul. He acknowledged no other mastership. No power of the world, no crowd insistence, no dictates of other men's opinions, could disturb him. "Henceforth let no man trouble me!" He had an inward confidence to which he could always resort. There in the secret shrine of his own soul, before the beautiful authority of Jesus, he bowed himself; and, fortified by that, went out unswervingly to face whatever the world might hold. Being committed there at the highest point of his devotion, he was set free from every lower thing.

We have considered thus two of the present-day

[22] Galatians 2:20. [23] Galatians 6:17.

tendencies with which the Christian gospel must deal:
the fatalistic idea of nature and the depreciation of human personality.* It remains that there should be brief
comment upon the third tendency, which at the beginning of this chapter was listed with the other two,
namely, the growing habit in our time of taking materialistic results as its estimate of success.

What this estimate is may be gathered almost anywhere in contemporary literature and in ordinary con-
versation. Success is playing the game in the way that
wins the fattest prize. Success is the big salary. Success is the thing that enables a man to live in a Park
Avenue penthouse apartment, to have a country estate
at the seashore and another in the mountains, to own a
fleet or two of automobiles and an airplane or two for
his children, and a yacht. Success is the thing that
writes a man's name in big type on the financial page,
and gives him power when the money magnates meet.
There is a fellowship of the stock market and of the
country club which believes in the orthodoxy of that
kind of success.

The Christian message has always come, and must
come with new decisiveness today, to cut clean across
the false direction of men's thinking. Before the face
of a society to whom success is selfishness it lifts up
the figure of one who came not to be ministered unto
but to minister. It points to Jesus of Nazareth, who
said to his disciples, "Whosoever will be chief among

you, let him be your servant." [24] It turns away from temporary false allurements toward those ultimate realizations which some day their souls must acknowledge. To an age which has shown its capacity to speak lies in place of truth, and to offer the false gold of quick advantage at the price of that inner wealth by which alone a man can live, the Christian gospel brings its clear corrective. It bids men see that there can never be any real success in an outward wealth which is bought by inner poverty. A penthouse apartment cannot lift a man's spirit out of the muck. Only the wings of the thoughts of God can do that. The greatest estate on the widest acres cannot expand an imagination which is chained to mean ambitions. Only a new consecration can do that. The swiftest seagoing yacht cannot carry a selfish man out toward a generous understanding of his world. Only a new heart can do that.

It is the business of the Christian religion to give men in this sense a new heart. Its destiny will depend upon its ability to do so. There are forces in the world today which are giving men new hearts. Some of these are dangerous forces which make men's hearts hot with the fierce pride of nationalism run rampant. Some of them have set men's hearts aflame with a new passion for social revolution as in Russia. Fires like these may burn out from the life of great nations much that has been dross. They may put an end, for a time at

[24] Matthew 20:27.

least, to cowardice, to social apathy, and to the individualism which seeks its own ends at the expense of the group. They may forge the metal of human life into a discipline and endurance which is hard as steel. They do lift men's ideas of success up above the mean and sordid personal shrewdness to the plane of a larger social hope. But the danger of some of these contemporary forces which are in part avowedly anti-christian, and which if, as in Italy, they are linked with ecclesiasticism, use it largely as a tool, is that their emphasis still is upon a conception of ultimate success which is won by the aggrandizement of one group, either class or nation, above the other competing groups of mankind. The idea of success that finds its inspiration in Christ is greater and more difficult. It lays upon the imagination and upon the wills of men the compulsion of so shaping their own purposes and the purposes of their group that these shall contribute to values by which the whole human family may be enriched. It is an ideal so great that no single individual can completely envisage it. It is so high that no one can hope to lift all the actuality of his life up to its level. But it does represent the aim which those who are mastered by the mind of Christ must never suffer themselves to lose. And the question which affects the present and future of Christianity is this: Is there enough dynamic in the Christian gospel as it is now accepted and understood to make men try to build a civilization in its spirit?

One thing which our time has demonstrated anew is the limitless power—it may be transfiguring, or it may be terrible—of a passionate conviction. When the World War began, Lenin was an exile in Switzerland, Trotsky was living from hand to mouth somewhere in a tenement of New York, Stalin was a prisoner in Siberia; but the conviction which these men had of a new order in Russia burned through every vast unlikelihood and was lifted presently like a torch above the ruins of a vanished era. Mussolini by his implacable conviction made himself master of Italy. Hitler, despised at first, and the leader of a little group of those who were accounted insignificant fanatics, gradually made the emotions of a great people cluster round himself because of the terrific intensity of his own belief which satisfied people's hunger for something that seemed sure. To what measure the ideas of these men, or any one of them, are right, only the longer judgment of history can fully tell; but this much is certain—they made millions *think* they were right, and they mobilized gigantic human powers because they were utterly committed to the thing that they believed. For the sake of it they would endure anything, persecution, postponement, imprisonment, the chance of death.

That is what the Christian spirit has also risen to in the times of its heroic manifestation. If it is to vindicate its heritage, it must do so now. There is need of Christian preachers who will interpret the mind of

Christ in terms of present facts. There is need of Christian men in business and in industry who at all immediate costs will be bent upon putting the spirit of Christ into those relationships in which the great multitude of human beings are involved. There is need of Christian statesmen who will lead their people to take the moral risks by which a Christian spirit may be made regulative in world affairs. These things will be costly. They will involve long hazards and present results which may seem like failure; but they blaze the road toward those hopes in which alone those who call themselves Christians can dare to find success.

CHAPTER VI

CHRISTIAN IDEALS CONFRONTING A RECALCITRANT WORLD

T HE mood of religious confidence has its climate of successive seasons, and they change as do the seasons of the earth. For a time it is summer, and the spirit moves through a realm of bright assurance where everything is blossoming. Then winter comes; and beliefs, which a little while before were golden with their fruit, now stand like stripped trees stark against the sunless sky.

As between the two, summer seems instinctively the more desirable; yet summer may be too opulent and too enervating. We can understand that now as we look back upon the period of what was called religious confidence—but which more truly might have been called complacency—in which a while ago we lived. Leibnitz once argued that this must be the best of all possible worlds because God, being all wise, must know all possibilities, and, being all powerful, must be able to create what He desires, and, being all good, must desire only the best. We may not have remembered this smooth academic logic of the philosopher, but we were disposed to reflect some of its easy confidence. If our world was not the best that could be imagined, nevertheless it seemed in many ways nearly good enough, and we were willing to assume that it would continually grow better.

In the Victorian era and in the early years of the present century there was much bland optimism abroad. The new doctrine of "progress" was proclaimed as though it gave benign assurance for the present and the future. Not only philosophers, but economists and business men and politicians, preened themselves with that smooth conviction. They thought that no rude winds of untoward forces would seriously ruffle the feathers of a prosperous and contented world. The poet laureate, Alfred Tennyson, was reflecting the hope which many held, even if he did not, when he wrote in *Locksley Hall Sixty Years After* of a time when the earth should see

"Every tiger madness muzzled, every serpent passion kill'd,
Every grim ravine a garden, every blazing desert till'd,
Robed in universal harvest up to either pole she smiles,
Universal ocean softly washing all her Warless Isles."

But the idea of easy automatic progress was roughly jolted by the World War. That war, in its outbreak and in its continuance, showed the anarchic passions in human individuals and in nations which can suddenly break through the crust of civilization like a volcano and spread the fires of savagery everywhere. Even then it was difficult for those who had been born in the nineteenth century, and had breathed its atmosphere, to realize the new climate of lowered confidence which was about to become prevailing. In the climax to his *Outline of History*, published in 1920, H. G. Wells was echoing the mood of earlier years when he wrote: "We know enough today to know that there is infinite room for betterment in every human concern. Nothing is needed but collective effort. Our poverty, our restraints, our infections and indigestions, our quarrels and misunderstandings, are all things controllable and removable by concerted human action." And after enumerating some of the amenities and luxuries of modern civilization, he goes on to say, "A time when all such good things will be for all men may be coming more nearly than we think. Each one who believes that brings the good time nearer; each heart that fails delays it."[1] That is to say, a little more intelligence, a little more benevolent emotion, and all will yet be well.

But more and more, even in the relatively favored nations, that cheerful confidence has begun to wane. The summer of serene expectancy has been succeeded by a winter of astringent scepticism. As Dean Inge has written in his caustic but witty way: "I repeat that there is no law of progress. Our future is in our own hands, to make or to mar. It will be an uphill fight to the end, and would we have it otherwise? Let no one suppose

[1] P. 593.

that evolution will ever exempt us from the struggles. 'You forget,' said the Devil, with a chuckle, 'that I have been evolving, too.' "[2]

It is not surprising that it should have been from Germany, where the tragic lessons of war itself were followed also by the bitter humiliation of defeat, that new and profound pessimism should appear. Spengler, in *The Decline of the West,* denied the idea of progress altogether, and represented human society as fated forever to move through its tragic cycles of promise and of partial fulfilment and then of decline and dissolution.

The sort of despair which Spengler set forth has been repudiated in action by a resurgent Germany; and to the religious spirit it was and is, on a deeper ground, intolerable. "It amounts," says Emil Brunner in his *Theology of Crisis,*[3] "to the decay of all spiritual substance. An age which has lost its faith in an absolute has lost everything. It must perish; it has no vitality left to pass the crisis; its end can only be—the end."

Yet the curious fact is that some of the most influential religious thinking of this time even in reacting against despair becomes itself almost despairing. Through its most passionate affirmations there sounds the inescapable note of crisis and catastrophe. Brunner is a disciple of Karl Barth, and Barth wins a dialectic victory for his faith largely by separating faith from

[2] In a symposium *Living Philosophies. A Series of Intimate Credos,* p. 317.
[3] P. 8.

the present world of stubborn fact. "How difficult it is," he says, "with pure heart and in awe of the Holy One, to take even the shortest step with Christ into society! . . . When we approach the execution of our program, we shall not be able . . . to reckon too soberly with 'reality'—our ideals being impossible and our goals unattainable."[4] Thus in great aspects of his theology, Barth would seem to be in flight from reality, if reality means this stubborn present world of ours which somehow must be dealt with. God's will is to be sought by the individual in an inner world of revelation. For the hurly-burly of everyday affairs religion has little relevance. The ancient dualism comes back, and business and industry and politics are regarded as the province of the Prince of this world, and therefore at last only a meaningless welter in which the spirit cannot be at home. God is to be found in those mystic apprehensions which make men feel the awful difference between religion and their ordinary reasonings. The world can go its own way toward whatever chance may await it; and none of these things matter to the ultimate well-being of the soul.

Here in America one of the most stimulating and provoking of contemporary thinkers is Reinhold Niebuhr. His influence among the younger intellectuals to whom he belongs, in widening circles of college under-

[4] *The Word of God and the Word of Man,* by Karl Barth, translated by Douglas Horton, pp. 278, 281.

graduates and in conferences of young people intent upon social change, has been great. He represents with outstanding clearness the reversal of the easy-going optimism which marked the generation now vanishing. In western Christendom until recently it was believed that the Kingdom of God might be in process of being planted here in the midst of the everyday life of earth. Men's minds, and the management of their affairs, could become by gradual evolution so steadily more Christian that presently our worst social evils might painlessly disappear. But against the bubble of this too hasty dream Niebuhr has flung the impact of his relentless realism. *Moral Man and Immoral Society* and *Reflections on the End of an Era* are the characteristic titles of his two best-known books; and in these books he draws a picture of society which is full of menace. In brief the convictions which he voices, and which he has led many of his generation to accept, are these: that there is an irreconcilable conflict between the ideals which individuals may hold and the more primitive and anarchic selfishness of men acting in the mass; that privileged groups will never willingly surrender their profitable power, and that the exploited multitudes, driven by the instinctive urge toward a larger life, are bound to break through the resistance of the privileged with revolutionary violence; that liberalism, both in social theory and in religion, has failed to understand the magnitude of these forces making for catastrophe; and that a high religion, recognizing "that pure love and disinterestedness are impossible of achievement[5] . . . must make present reality bearable even while it insists that God is denied, frustrated and defied in the immediate situation."[6]

Plainly in this there is no smooth counsel; it is a prophecy through which sound the forewarning of the bells of judgment, if not of doom. There is an echo of a mood almost as somber as that of Spengler in Niebuhr's words concerning the modern capitalistic order: "Destined to premature decay, it dreamed of progress almost until the hour of dissolution";[7] and "the enterprises of collective man, his social orders, his empires and civilizations must die a sanguinary death."[8]

And an able young scholar of that generation among whom Niebuhr has won so many hearers has written:

"It can fairly be said that we are living in an age strangely akin to the apocalyptic age of Palestine. The cry, 'This is the end of the era' travels like the wind through the broad stretches of the land. The expectation of disaster broods over many parts of the country, and apprehension for the future stultifies the activities of men. In other quarters the mood is one of brighter hope and anticipation. But whatever the nuances may be, the central theme is the same—the darkness is deepening, the end is not far off. Here and there men and

[5] *Reflections on the End of an Era*, p. 279.
[6] *Ibid.*, p. 282. [7] *Ibid.*, p. 3. [8] *Ibid.*, p. 18.

women frantically try to drown their anxiety in hysterical excitement, while others go through the gathering clouds, grim and mute. The time is waxing late." [9]

When winter deepens, it is hard sometimes to visualize the return of spring. When the mood of spiritual confidence sinks to doubt or near-despair, it is hard to feel that it will come back to joyous blossoming. But spring does follow winter nevertheless; and while it is winter, much useful pruning can be done. While the sap is *not* running, the trees of many kinds of fruitfulness may be shaped for a future harvest. So, with religion, the seasons of scepticism can be used to cut off the barren branches, and to make the central stock of conviction stronger thereby. Christian thinking today may well go through this wholesome surgery. It should be definitely recognized that Christian ethics will not work out through the smooth processes once expected. There will have to be new recognition of the intractable forces in this world, and of the heavy cost of overcoming them. It must be perceived that men are often swayed less by reason than by instinctive passion, and that great social changes may come through processes of violence which idealists would not choose. And it must be understood that the apocalyptic note, never absent from New Testament Christianity, must come back again into ours, with its warning of crisis and suffer-

[9] From *First and Last Things,* a thesis by Theodore P. Ferris of General Theological Seminary.

ing before anything resembling the Kingdom of God
can appear.

With all this, then, in the background of our present
consciousness, we may well try to build up against it
the framework of a Christian ethic strong enough to
stand the testing of these times.

Its first emphasis will be upon the fact of God. Re-
peatedly in these chapters we have remembered this
truth that all belief, and all prevailing effort, must be
founded upon something deeper than humanism, deeper
than all resources inherent in our unrelated selves. The
evils and difficulties of these days can be met victori-
ously only by men who are stayed upon an infinite reliance. Sturdy old Brother Lawrence, who has enriched
the devotional life of many by his *Practice of the Presence of God,* put the truth in robust and homely way
when he told his friend, Monsieur Beaufort,

"That when an occasion of practising some virtue
offered he addressed himself to God, saying, *'Lord, I
cannot do this unless thou enablest me,'* and that he
then received strength more than sufficient.

"That when he had failed in his duty, he only con-
fessed his fault, saying to God, *'I shall never do other
wise if you leave me to myself; 'tis you must hinder my
falling and mend whatever is amiss.'* That after this
he gave himself no further uneasiness about it."[10]

[10] P. 8.

All vital Christian life, both in its ethical standards and in its dynamic power, must rest upon this sense of the reality and primacy of the grace of God.

The Christian believes that he is not left to his own devices in determining what ultimately is right or wrong, practicable or impracticable. His business is not only as a realist to study this world's complicated facts. His business is to recognize among these and above these the one Fact which is visible only to those who have the spiritual eyes that see. It was not one biased toward religion, but a keen observer of life and an incisive critic of contemporary literature who has written: "Light will finally come if only the man dedicate the whole of his deeper being to the end of attaining to truth. Blindness is ultimately of the soul, vision the fruit, not merely of cerebration, but of sincere aspiration." [11] And again he wrote of the fact that the man who seeks goodness finds that he is allied with "Something other than himself—*quelque chose en moi qui soit plus moi-même que moi*—and that by . . . merging into that Something he can attain to release, tranquillity, and joy." [12] There is a will of God which is righteousness and rightness; and His will, if we can discover it, is our peace.

This perception of the will of God is not always by analysis. It does not lead at once to a map-making of

[11] *The Prospects of Humanism,* by Lawrence Hyde, p. 57.
[12] *Ibid.,* p. 87.

all the way ahead. It is an intuition that foreshadows the direction in which to go. It is like the pointing of a compass which indicates that the pole is this way rather than another. But it is also more than that. It is a consciousness of companionship. It is a feeling that when one walks in the suggested way he walks with the infinite Pathfinder who knows the end from the beginning and whose guidance can be trusted, no matter how long may be the road.

It is true of course that many who have wanted to find a workable system of ethics for the world they live in have resisted this belief of religion that it has some sort of supernatural contact which gives it guidance. They have felt indignantly that religion evades the labor of dealing directly with facts by this claim of having an esoteric authority not subject to the review of ordinary common sense. And often this feeling of theirs has had much reason on its side. For the intuitions of religion have been hardened into ecclesiastical orthodoxies. Earnest but dull-witted scribes have taken the flashing perceptions of the seers and prophets and tried to reduce them to a system; and then have claimed a sacrosanct authority for the system they have worked out. By this means so-called Christian ethics has been taken away from the wholesome stimulus and corrective of unfolding life. It became unreasonable because it was unrelated. It demanded recognition because of the source it said it came from, like inadequate descendants of a great family demanding recognition for nothing but their birth. Thus popes by their bulls and church councils by their pronouncements have laid down laws for belief and conduct which were deduced at second hand from assumptions which sounded like religion, and which used the name of God to browbeat and silence any further thinking. That sort of stereotyping of ethics in the name of orthodoxy is manifestly an evil. The ecclesiastical conjurers who try to produce results by formulas are like the exorcists told of in the book of Acts who tried to cast out evil spirits through adjuring them "by Jesus whom Paul preacheth," [13]— with results disastrous to themselves. They had no power because they had no first-hand knowledge.

Yet their imitation was a tribute to a power that did exist. The deeper reality must not be lost because of its abuse. All the efforts—even the clumsy and unsuccessful efforts—to produce codes which can then be enforced as Christian ethics are testimony to the fact that in ethical judgments reached through contact with the living God there is a sureness and power which no others can duplicate. Still above the crowding facts rises the Fact; and when any man's soul has surely seen it, then all other shining points in the sky of his understanding take their relationship from that, as the stars are seen as east or west according to their relation to the polar star. The maps of the moral con-

[13] Acts 19:13.

stellations which men make in the name of religion
may often be inaccurate, and will need continually to
be reviewed in the light of growing knowledge; but
religion can never flinch from the conviction born of
high experience that it can bring to all human ethics
the incomparable gift of its eternal centering. For
the religious man, the light that is here to guide life
is not produced in him; it shines through him. The
sense of direction of which his soul is conscious even
when immediate issues are obscure seems to him something more than the result of his thinking. It is his
own thought working upon, and guided by, an influence that streams upon him direct from God, as the
radio-beam comes to the master of the ocean-liner
through the fog, and shows him the direction which
all his seamanship then must be alert to follow. So it
is that the religious man has a quality of confidence
which the man who is trying to fashion an ethic without religion lacks. In the words of Phillips Brooks:
"It is the result of some great experience in the life
of a man that it makes him a purer medium through
which the highest truth shines on other men. Henceforth, he is altered; he becomes tenderer, warmer,
richer; he seems to be full of truths and revelations
which he easily pours out. Now you not merely see
him, you see through him to things behind. It is not
that he has learned some new facts, but the very substance of the man is altered, so that he stands no

longer as a screen, but as an atmosphere through which the eternal truths come to you all radiant."

The second emphasis which enters into all Christian judgments is reverence for personality. This is something far deeper and stronger than a general humanitarianism. There may be a humanitarian *respect* for personality, a polite and mild well-wishing which serves for ordinary times; but this respect is not the same thing as *reverence*. Reverence for personality must be grounded upon religion. It is only when man is seen in relation to the greatness of God that the freedom of his personality is accounted so infinite a thing as to be worth unlimited defense.

The difference may be seen vividly exemplified in Germany of this present time. There a new philosophy of the absolute state has demanded the unquestioning subordination and conformity of the individual. There is to be a totalitarian authority and a totalitarian idea. The mind and conscience of the particular person must surrender to the corporate power.

It is significant to observe which possible forces have and which have not combated this degradation of personality. The ruthless suppression of individual freedom, and the regimentation of thought into an iron pattern of political dictation, are deadly to all creative art, to truth-seeking science, and to unfettered scholarship in so far as these should dare touch the realities of life.

But it has not been from the artists, nor from the scientists, nor from the faculties of universities, that heroic and sustained protest has chiefly come. *Their* respect for personality turns out, under pressure, to be too academic to be resolute. It can change and conform itself to new necessities. Since the value of personality is regarded as a mere human conception, it can be suavely twisted into adjustment to an authority which claims to confer a favor on people by taking their personalities away. But there is in Germany another group which does not so easily abandon its convictions. Thousands of pastors and people in the German Evangelical Church have refused to surrender their liberty of conscience, and have dared to proclaim the truth as they see it, full in the face of attempted tyranny. They—and only they effectively—have resisted the indiscriminate persecution of Jews, have refused to take unqualified oaths of allegiance to political and ecclesiastical dictators, and have maintained the sovereignty of the spirit as against the pronouncements of the state. On Sunday, March 10, 1935, there was read from hundreds of pulpits in Germany a manifesto of the Confessional Synod which declared:

"We see for our people a deadly danger. This danger consists of the new religion.

"The first commandment states: "Thou shalt have no other gods before Me.' The new religion is disobedient to this first commandment.

"Through this religion a racial and nationalist view of life has become a creed. Through it blood and race, people, honor and liberty have been raised to the level of divinity.

"Faith in an eternal Germany, which the new religion requires, has been put in the place of faith in an eternal kingdom of our Saviour, Jesus Christ. . . .

"Whoever places blood, race, and nationality in place of God, the Creator, destroys the State's foundations. . . .

"Therefore the church dares not bow blindly to the totalitarian demands of the State which the new religion has created. Bound to God's word, it is her duty to witness the omnipotence of Jesus Christ, who alone is empowered to bind and relieve human conscience. To Him alone is given all power in heaven and earth." [14]

And in June, 1934, at its organization the Confessional Synod had proclaimed:

"God, through Jesus Christ, claims our whole life. The heresy is refuted that there can be spheres of life in which we do not belong to Him, but to other masters." [15]

There is expressed both the paradox and the power

[14] *Federal Council Bulletin,* published by the Federal Council of the Churches of Christ in America. New York, May, 1935.
[15] *The Church—State Struggle in Germany,* by Henry Smith Leiper, p. 6. Published by American Section: Universal Christian Council for Life and Work.

of that freedom of personality which the Christian claims. He will not be subject to lesser masters in any way which conflicts with that higher mastery which has set him free. He will not admit the right of any forces to cripple the growth of the soul which is accountable to God.

It must be understood that a Christian ethic, holding at its heart a reverence for human personality as a thing divine, will not win its way in the contemporary world by any smooth assertion. It must gird itself for costly struggle. As Nicholas Berdyaev has written:

"Democratic and socialized humanism ceases to be concerned with man, it is interested in the structure of society; but is not interested in the inner life of man. Such is the fatal process. . . . The destiny of man is infinitely more complicated than men supposed in the nineteenth century. The reorganized world is moved by other values than the value of man, or the value of truth—by such values as the power of technics, race, nationality, the state, class, collectivity. The will to truth is vanquished by the will to power. The dialectic of this process is very subtle. Man desires power, power of his own, but this leads to his exalting power above himself, above man, to his being ready in the name of his power to sacrifice his own humanity. Power is objectified, and abstracted from human existence. The value of the power of technics, of the power of the state, of the power of race, of the power of class, bestializes man; in the name of these powers it is permissible to perpetrate any cruelty whatever upon man. . . .

"There are, then, a multitude of forces at work tending to dehumanize man, to make of him either the image and likeness of nature, as in Romanticism, or the image and likeness of the machine. But man is meant to be neither; he is the image and likeness of God."[16]

It is only in this conviction of man as "the image and likeness of God" that reverence for personality can have dynamic power. Without an infinite anchorage, a mere humanistic respect for personality disintegrates before economic and political ruthlessness. But Christian ethics must maintain the supremacy of personality, or lose its own soul. It must defend the minority, and the unpoplar individual, against oppression. It must champion free speech and civil liberties, because only in the atmosphere of these can free souls breathe. And it must dedicate itself to the building up of a social order in which what happens to man and not what piles up money shall be the supreme consideration. As E. Stanley Jones has memorably written: "Christianity will fit better into a co-operative order than into a competitive order. It is not at home in an order where the weakest go to the wall and the devil takes the hindmost. In such

16 "The Breakdown of the Humanistic Theory of Progress," translated from the Russian by William H. Dunphy in *The Living Church*, pp. 97, 98, January 26, 1935. By permission of the Morehouse Publishing Co.

a society Christianity is gasping for breath. It is not its native air. But its genius would flower in a co-operative order, for there love and good will and sharing, which are of the very essence of Christianity, should be at home." [17]

Principles such as these are no glittering generalities. They have to do with hard, defiant facts. They mean that Christians must take up the sword of the spirit against many contemporary tyrannies, of which capitalism, fascism, and communism alike are guilty. The whole Christian Church ought to feel outraged when organized injustice or mob-passion overrides and browbeats the personality of the disadvantaged man—when cotton mill strikers in Marion, North Carolina, or miners in Harlan County, Kentucky, are brutally put to silence and denied effective appeal to the outside world, when negroes in Scottsboro, Alabama, are convicted on testimony which would never have held against a white man, when advocates of disarmament are threatened by the truculent "patriots" of the American Legion, and when millions of men and women and children are suffering the cruelties of an economic order which is more concerned with profits for the masters than with what happens to the personalities of the people.

There is no disguising the fact that if Christianity dares to take seriously its own inescapable conviction of the sovereign importance of personality, it will come

---

[17] *Christ's Alternative to Communism,* p. 32.

into collison with the social order as it exists today. Paul Hutchinson has set at least part of the truth in sharp distinctness when in *The Ordeal of Western Religion* he wrote:

"Western religion finds itself in growing tension with Western society. . . . This tension, at bottom, rests on an assumption. . . . The assumption is that of the supreme worth of the individual." [18]

"But is not the time here to ask whether such a claim has any relevancy to the modern world? Defend it as an ideal if you will. But can an ideal which is impossible of controlling action, or a proposition which is beyond proof, have value? And this notion of the supreme worth of the individual is as far beyond any realization today as Einstein's mathematics is beyond the use of the paper-hanger measuring off the wall-paper in my living-room. Mind, I am not now passing judgment on the religious intuition which has produced this idea. Mr. Joseph Wood Krutch, and a good many others, think they are justified, for biological and related reasons, in holding the very conception of the supreme worth of the individual to be nonsense. But without going off the deep end into the philosophic despair which leads Mr. Krutch to conclude that 'there is no reason to suppose that (man's) own life has any more meaning than the life of the humblest insect that crawls from one annihilation to another,' this much I do assert—that no social

[18] P. 57. By permission of Houghton Mifflin Company.

system now known or contemplated offers the slightest comfort to this doctrine of individual importance." [19]

"When religion, therefore, comes forward with the claim that its principal mission is to champion the supreme worth of the individual, it should be forced either to provide blueprints of a social order in which the individual would be given supreme worth—a requirement that I, for one, am persuaded is beyond meeting—or to recognize the irrelevancy of its approach to modern society." [20]

The swinging confidence of those words makes them sound at first convincing; and there is clear truth in them. It is true that religion has no right to speak in vaporous imaginings. It must make its ideals walk the earth in perceivable shape if they are to be taken seriously. But it is fallacious to represent an ideal to be followed as though it must be the same thing as an accomplished fact. Religion does not become irrelevant simply because its ideals are admittedly still in process of being realized.

A truly Christian ethic might be irrelevant to the existing social order, but not for the reason which Paul Hutchinson suggests. It will seem irrelevant to those who have no belief in the power of the spirit; and it will be *kept* irrelevant, if they can manage it, by those among our economic and financial masters who secretly dread

[19] *Ibid.*, pp. 59, 60.   [20] *Ibid.*, p. 61.

the power of the spirit, and are on guard lest this power be released. There are many who want no social message of religion, and ask vehemently for what they call the "simple gospel," by which they mean a gospel denatured of its disturbing implications. They want to keep Christianity as a detached mood for special times and places; and they say that modern civilization could not have been built on any such foundation as the words of Jesus. That may be true. But they do not go on to recognize that what *might* be built upon his words could be a better thing than modern civilization is. They do not wish to take that risk, and so they prefer to think that in everyday concerns Christianity is irrelevant.

But suppose Christianity recognizes its heroic task to introduce into the present social order enough divine discontent and enough dynamic to begin to destroy its present evils in order that something nobler may be builded in its place. Will it then be "irrelevant" if it cannot "provide blueprints" of what the new social order is to be? To suppose that is to make the obvious mistake of ignoring the difference between the organic and the mechanical. A new life-principle does not unfold according to "blueprints." Creative ideals at work among men do not click like cogs of a machine. But the reality of these ideals is no less powerful for the fact that they develop in manifold and spontaneous ways. Love is an ideal which makes a group of individuals into a family and a bare house into a home; but nobody can blueprint that family's relationships from day to day. Similarly the Christian reverence for personality as seeking embodiment in the whole social order cannot be exactly charted in advance. Even to attempt that is to misconceive the function of the spirit. This is to inspire, not to specify. Whenever religion tries to lay down an exact political or social program, it only creates another theocracy in which the ideal becomes petrified in the imperfect form. Often the business of religion is to increase and not to allay the tension between the ideal and the present fact. It points to goals which are bound to be unattainable in any near time. It creates an inner unrest which is endlessly provocative. "One must have chaos within one to give birth to a dancing star." [21]

But no one who considers history will suppose that because the ideal does not produce an immediate program it is therefore powerless. The Christian reverence for personality is no new thing in the world; and though its working has been hindered by ignorance and evil, it is never halted. The ethical demands which the Christian ideal has continually made have broken one bondage after another in which human personalities were enslaved. In the beginning of the Christian era slavery was an almost universal fact; in the feudal ages, the peasant was little better than the chattel of his lord; a century ago agricultural laborers in Great Britain who dared to organize to ask for higher pay were sent on

[21] *Thus Spoke Zarathustra,* by Friedrich Nietzsche, Part I, A.

convict ships to penal servitude. The recognition of the right of every personality is far from perfect now; but only a stubborn blindness could fail to recognize the forces working today, wherever there is enlightened Christianity, toward a more abundant life for every individual.

If every individual should attain abundant life, and attain it in a fellowship ruled by Jesus' law of love, then that would mean that here on this earth the Kingdom of God had come. The Kingdom of God, of course, is the ultimate goal of Christian hope and Christian effort. To introduce into all life those principles which are consistent with God's Kingdom is the motive of Christian ethics.

But when and where can the Kingdom of God be realized? Is it in any real sense a possibility here in this tough, actual world? Or is it only a far-off vision to be left as an apocalyptic dream?

There has always been a conflict of thought about this. There is a conflict now. In the Gospels, there are traditions in which Jesus is remembered to have taught of the Kingdom as the leaven of a spirit already transformingly at work; and there are other traditions in which he seems to picture the Kingdom as the miraculous creation of a new heaven and a new earth. Shall the Kingdom be striven for, or must it only be waited for? That is the practical question. Nobody believes today that the Kingdom will come as smoothly as many in former decades were fain to suppose. All serious students of fact admit that it will be only through crisis that we can win through to any social order in which the will of God, and the values of Christ, could be prevailing. But many others think that not even crisis can do it. The contrast is expressed in a curiously illuminating way by the contemporary words of two ministers and teachers of the same Christian communion. Said one of them: "A revolutionary, preaching the abundant life for all—that's my Jesus—One who revealed it to be God's will that a Divine Society should be established here upon earth." [22] The other said: "There is really no such thing as progress. A social order comes up, flourishes, declines and disintegrates, or is destroyed. But a remnant of the righteous is saved and that remnant brings in a new order, which breeds its own evils, sometimes worse than those they supersede. The idea that sacrifice and suffering today can be endured or even rejoiced in because as a result the day after tomorrow the Millennium will be ushered in, is all bosh. There is neither history nor religion in it. Sacrifice and suffering are religious because through them we attain spiritual truth." [23]

If this latter view were true, then religion would have to dissolve into other-worldliness altogether. This world,

[22] William B. Spofford in *The Witness,* February 28, 1935.
[23] Bernard Iddings Bell, quoted in *The Southern Churchman,* February 16, 1935.

and all the effort to establish righteousness within it, would be a shadow-show. Nothing would matter except the hidden inner life which detaches itself from the turbulent realities of every day, and finds its solace in the cloudy arcana of Barthian contemplation, or in the mystery of the Mass. The Kingdom of God may come in some transcendent realm; but not now, and never here.

Such a surrender of the more virile and courageous religious hope would destroy the glory of the Christian message. It would turn the trumpet into a plaintive flute. Christianity cannot prevail by a message of escape. Its Master dared to say "I have overcome the world";[24] and the world is not overcome by flight from it, no matter how high-sounding may be the words in which that flight should be expressed. Christianity must keep, and the Christian pulpit must proclaim, a gospel which believes that here and now there are approximations to God's Kingdom great enough to be fought for, and real enough to be served as though they would come true.

That is the way the prophets preached. They knew the stubborn evil of the actual world. They knew how far off is any completed Kingdom of God. But they believed that God was working in history, and that evil and injustice would be destroyed, and goodness exalted into power.

[24] St. John 16:33.

This sort of valiant commitment to the Kingdom of God ought to be the note of all contemporary preaching. Granted that much of our society still is pagan. Granted that the ideal of love as a determining factor in social change is often weak and insufficient. Nevertheless, in some true measure at least, it is there; and the Christian gospel of the Incarnation holds that the power of love, which is the power of God, can increasingly take possession of human personalities and make them capable of ideals and efforts which uninspired nature scoffs at as impossible. The Christian gospel ought to ring with the incredible confidence of the prophets. It ought to proclaim again that "the mountain of the Lord's house . . . shall be exalted above the hills, and all the nations shall flow into it." [25] And it ought to point out, in the face of the moral pessimism of this time, that already there are those who do set their faces toward the purpose of God as revealed in Jesus and say "he will teach us of his ways, and we will walk in his paths." [26]

It is the fashion now-a-days to decry the religious liberalism which has believed that our social order could be made better by a gradual and gracious change. That liberalism—as we have already recognized—was too easy-going and too optimistic. But there is no need of swinging to an opposite and fanatical extreme, and declaring that no forces can be effective except those which rise out of the violence of men's explosive pas-

[25] Isaiah 2:2.   [26] Isaiah 2:3.

sions. • The Christian preacher must not forget that there is such a thing as spiritual leaven which can work until much is leavened. He must not forget that there is a seed growing secretly, and that out of it great things can come. His first business is to put into the hearts of individual men and women the disturbing and expansive suggestions of Christ; and he will see that when these take root they may, like other growing things, split resistances which are hard as rock.•

A Christian social order is best foretokened by men and women who in an order confessedly materialistic are at least trying to be Christian. Such there have been and are in every community. Through the dark years of economic depression there have been men who as owners or executives in industry have cut their own salaries, abandoned their own profits and jeopardized their possessions in order to keep employment for their workers. There have been women who have reduced their scale of living rather than insist on payment of mortgage interest when they knew that insistence might turn some struggling debtor out of a home. And there have been those who have allied themselves with the unemployed and the underprivileged to help win for them the advantages which they themselves did not lack. As these words are written, there comes a letter from a girl who went not long ago into an industrially backward state to be a teacher in a school for workers' children. She writes:

"You must excuse my bad typing, for I am in bed for a bit, getting my very insignificant leg wound healed. I am none the worse for it, since the bullet did not touch the bone and has given me an opportunity to reach people—much more useful than getting in jail." Then she goes on to describe how she had been hurt. A delegation from the school had come down to a neighboring town where there had been a strike against a textile mill. "Our good friend the Methodist minister here, who has been pivotal in the whole strike, and enabled it to succeed here without violence of any kind, has been our chief host, although we have been living in strikers' homes. Our part in the parade was to help lead songs, etc. The minister himself went around among the men and felt them for guns, so we knew beyond any possible doubt that we were unarmed. Three hundred were women. Even the sheriff says no shots came from our side."

But as they marched past the mill, they were fired upon from the mill windows. And then the account proceeds:

"While the wounded were being taken to the hospital, and the sheriff locked up the entire mill force who refused to give up arms, the paraders rallied round their leaders, and, following the advice of the minister, who has played an important part in the strike, decided not to get guns, but to send in a message that if those in the mill would throw their weapons into the yard and promise to close the mill they would be allowed to go home unmolested."

That is only a tiny vignette from a picture which is being painted on a huge and ominous canvas. At innumerable points in our present-day industrial order there are collisions between employers and employees, with a mounting danger of bitterness, estrangement, and violence. A stark conflict between two self-interests each blindly hostile to the other would lead, of course, to some sort of result, but never to a result that could be Christian. Into the struggle there must be introduced the spirit of those who are not seeking to gain but to give. There must be many others who, like the girl who marched with the unarmed strikers, and like the minister who kept an industrial struggle from flaming into violence, are willing to be wounded in order that a larger justice and brotherhood may somehow emerge.

It is here that the Christian pulpit must make unmistakably plain the compulsion of the spirit of Christ. If he were standing in the midst of our modern civilization, we cannot doubt the values for which he would stand. He would recognize the beauty and worth in the great structure which our material achievements have built up. But he would look deeper. He would not be satisfied with limited and unequal aspects of prosperity. He would be concerned to know what was happening to the multitudes of the people. He would be sensitive to injustice, and instinctively he would champion the weak.

Many who are living today have heard the voice of one of the great prophets of our generation, a man who almost more than any one of his contemporaries seemed to be aflame with the spirit of Christ, and one who, although he died young, will be remembered longer than most of those who have grown old, Studdert Kennedy. He burned his life out in the intensity of his effort to make men see what a Christian civilization ought to mean. He used to say that he had "a passion of pity for the poor"; and because he did have that, those who listened to him, of every rank and class, felt the unearthly power of his blazing message. They knew that he reached down under all accidents of circumstance or possession and yearned to touch and help the needy man. Under his spell people began to be aware of human truths which are deeper than all class divisions. The man or woman of privilege wanted to get loose from exploiting selfishness. The man or woman on whom life had borne hard felt the inward bitterness begin to melt. Christian preachers of today, if they are to make the gospel of Jesus powerful, must feel and communicate something of that same "passion of pity for the poor." It can, of course, be a terrible thing, formidable as a flaming sword. It can rouse malignant hostility among those who do not want to face it. It may prove unhappily the blade of separation among some nominal church members. But it can redeem the Church. The great prophets had this pity. Elijah had it. Amos had it. Isaiah had it. Above all, Jesus had it. And in this living time, unless the preachers who pretend to speak in his name are to be as "sounding brass or a tinkling cymbal," [27] this pity of his for the poor, a pity interpreted into the realities of social righteousness, must speak again.

But this, of course, as many an urgent social reformer will point out, is not enough. Merely to speak idealistic words in the face of a social and economic order which is fundamentally cruel will not let the oppressed go free. No, not yet; but it is a beginning. The Christian pulpit in its honest utterance Sunday by Sunday is no small power in lighting in men's souls the disturbing flame of a new social conscience, which when it is once roused is not easy to quench. As Dean Gauss of Princeton has written in *A Primer for Tomorrow:* "If we would keep our culture healthy we must find a new and more difficult world to conquer and the only such world is the inner world of man's spirit. . . . The only impediment to the extension of commodious living to all men is the recalcitrant spirit of man himself and this now is the last redoubt which we must storm." [28] The word of the preacher may help to storm this redoubt of men's unwillingness to listen; and then there waits the next stage of Christian strategy in making a more Christian social order possible.

This next stage is the formulation of the principles

in the light of which such a new order may be built. It
will not be the specific function of the Church to provide a series of blueprints—to use again the word upon
which Paul Hutchinson insisted. Economists and tech-
nicians must work out the details of these. But the
Christian Church can show broad lines upon which a
better social order must be drawn if it is to be expansive
enough to give room for the souls of men. It must put
forth its social creed, and that is exactly what the Christian Church, through different denominational bodies,
and through larger federations, has been doing with an
increasing convergence of agreement. The pronouncements of the Federal Council of the Churches of Christ
in America, the statements formulated by the Conference
of Jewish Rabbis, the resolutions passed by many denominational gatherings, and in part at least the en-
cyclical *Quadragesimo Anno* of Pope Pius Eleventh,
come close together in the supreme emphases which they
demand for the architecture of the social and economic
system which must replace our present confusion. Their
essential message was expressed in the joint appeal entitled *The Present Crisis as a Summons to Spiritual Advance,* formulated and put forth in January, 1934, by the
spokesmen for thirty national Christian communions in
America.

"We Are Agreed," they wrote, "in thinking of our
present breakdown as not merely economic but spiritual.
Our new powers of machine industry and our unrivalled

technical skill have failed because they have been controlled by the motive of private acquisitiveness instead of public service. The attainment of economic health cannot come from a mere return to things as they were. We should regard it as a dire tragedy if a mild recovery should now blind our eyes to the moral issues involved and lull our consciences into complacency with our former condition."

It then insists upon fundamental changes. . . . *"We Are Agreed* that our emphasis on spiritual values calls for a rebuilding of our economic life. Private profit as the cornerstone of the economic order appeals to men to be selfish when the Christian Gospel bids them be unselfish and seek the common good. We plead, therefore, for a courageous facing of the cause and cure of our present situation in terms of the Christian principle that the aim of any economic system should be the welfare of the people." [29]

And as an example of the sort of declarations which are being made by Christian communions severally, there may well be recorded what the General Council of Congregational Churches in the United States said at its national assembly at Oberlin, Ohio, in June, 1934.

After a review of contemporary facts concerning "our present competitive profit-seeking economy," it went on to say:

[29] *The Present Crisis as a Summons to Spiritual Advance.* The Federal Council of the Churches of Christ in America, January, 1934.

"These flagrant social evils exist side by side with potential natural abundance, which the present economy is unable to utilize and distribute, however much good it may have done in the past and however honest and idealistic individuals dependent upon the system may be."

Then the Council resolved—

"That we set ourselves to work toward:

"The abolition of the system responsible for these destructive elements in our common life by eliminating the system's incentives and habits, the legal forms which sustain it, and the moral ideals which justify it.

"The inauguration of a genuinely co-operative social economy democratically planned to adjust production to consumption requirements, to modify or eliminate private ownership of the means of production or distribution wherever such ownership interferes with the social good.

"And . . . we encourage the study by our local churches of these and related economic problems for their social and moral implications." [30]

That last paragraph is important. Good intentions, if they are vague intentions, cannot make the Church powerful for social transformation. Individualistic piety coupled with social ignorance equals zero, so far as any contribution toward the Kingdom of God is concerned. There is no use wishing for a better world un-

[30] *The Christian Century*, April 17, 1935, p. 502.

less there is clear-sighted effort to discover the way toward it. If the Church is to play an effective part in
social advance, it ought to kindle aspiration, but equally
it ought to encourage education. Too much preaching
is discredited as wordy rhetoric because it merely vocif-
erates a demand for smooth perfection without revealing any intelligent understanding of the difficulties
which existing economic and social facts present, nor
any awareness of the kind of practical choices by which
alone these can be dealt with. In regard to the difficulties, it would be well if every thoughtful Christian could
ponder not only what Reinhold Niebuhr has written,
but also such an analysis as that set forth by Harold J.
Laski in *The State in Theory and Practice;* and along
with that let him then read the equally able and more
constructive study by F. Ernest Johnson entitled *The
Church and Society.* The unusual importance of this
book lies in its just and discerning insistence upon both
of two values which are often pulled apart by rival emphases. It maintains a faith in moral factors in social
change—the faith which *Moral Man and Immoral Society* seems to abandon to despair; and at the same time,
it compels consideration of the sort of works without
which this faith is dead.

"The often repeated assertion," writes Ernest Johnson, "that resistance to the socialization of wealth and
unwillingness on the part of the privileged to relinquish
their advantages may be taken for granted, and that

therefore violent revolution is inevitable, runs counter
to the insistence of social Christianity that collective
human nature, so to say, is redeemable. One contention
can no more be proved than the other—except by the
event. . . . It often happens that the old adage, 'Necessity is the mother of invention,' acquires a moral significance—when the necessity is moral. The mere
pressure of a 'Thou shalt' may release the inventiveness
to convert it into a 'Thou canst'!"

Then with equal weight he goes on to say: "But much
moral ineptitude is occasioned by a failure to link up
motivation and technique. I doubt very much whether
the campaign of 1923 against the twelve-hour day in
steel would have borne fruit had not the existence of
an available technique been somewhat dramatically dis-
closed. To stir up emotions when there is no way out,
to arouse expectations without a technique for their
realization, is not a moral but an immoral proceeding.
The increased emphasis within the church on moral
education is equivalent to recognition that techniques
of living, for the individual and for the group, are within the sphere of the church's responsibility." [31]

Yet it is true, of course, that there are those who will
still hold that the educative processes, and the moral and
spiritual influences which try to bring about conversion

[31] *The Church and Society,* by F. Ernest Johnson, pp. 70, 104.
By permission of the Abingdon Press. Copyright, 1935.

in men's social attitudes, cannot prevail. Men like Rein-hold Niebuhr may continue to insist that the forces of intelligence and conscience are not strong enough for the grim realities which face us. They believe that the fairer industrial and economic system which ought to come and must come will be brought to pass largely by the terrible mass demands of exploited men, embittered by what they believe to be long injustice, and scornful of the influence of religion which seems to them too slow and too feeble to work the transformation they demand.

Then Christian preachers must be ready to interpret the possible truth embodied here. There may have to be an apocalyptic element in our future. That is to say, we may have to pass through a period when the dark forces of convulsion will be God's necessary process of purging away some of the ancient evils of the world. Then supremely there will be needed a spiritual insight and a far-seeing discrimination between things that appear to be religious and those cataclysmic events in which the moving forces of God may actually be present.

An illustration of this difference is at our doors now in Mexico. The picture of conditions there seems on the surface to present an unreasonable persecution of religion. Many people both in Mexico and in this country would feel that to defend Christianity they must defend the interests of the organized Christian Church; but, as a matter of fact, the Church which has been dominant in Mexico has largely failed in its opportunity toward the people. Together with those elements in its life which are noble, the Church of Rome in many lands presents one aspect which often is dangerous, and sometimes in the long run destructive both to itself and to the life surrounding. It tends to identify the interests of the organization with the ideals of the Kingdom of God, and to assume that the Kingdom advances if the organization is clothed with prestige and power. In this grave error it is conspicuous but not solitary. In lesser degree all ecclesiastical bodies may represent the working of the same temptation. They may build up their own emoluments at the expense of the general good. Therefore all organized Christianity everywhere may well consider what Bishop Creighton from the vantage-point of his own life and work in Mexico has written concerning what has happened there. "The strident secular State is a direct reaction from a theocracy which makes the Church an end in itself, devoting itself to its own aggrandizement at the expense of the humanity which it is divinely commissioned to inspire and save. The Church has no business to grow rich and powerful while its faithful grovel in unspeakable poverty and abysmal ignorance. It cannot escape from the dictum of its divine Head. It is created to spend and be spent, not to accumulate and grow rich. Either it lives by giving its life, or it dies in withholding it. The

Church in its mission to mankind has a direct social obligation. If it does not fulfil it, it deserves its fate if it is eliminated." [32]

Now that the deep instinct of the multitude for a larger life is breaking through into expression, it is taking forms hostile to the Church as this has been predominantly known in Mexico. In so far as those forms are indiscriminate and unreasonable, they are a hurt both to the present and to the future; but, nevertheless, the preponderance of the values of God may lie at this moment not with the institution which bears His name, but with that fierce up-surge of the soul of man where God *is* even at the moment when blindly He is denied.

Here in America in the days to come there will be needed prophets who can see beneath the show of things. The realities of God are not fenced in by the ecclesiastical structure. The Church may have to suffer if it cannot see the judgment coming upon its world. There must be men who know for themselves, and help their people increasingly to understand, that the Kingdom of God is greater and more creative than its supposed embodiments. Men now in the ranks of labor and not bishops in cathedrals may be the authentic builders of the highroad for the new entrance into our life of what some day will be the more evident spirit of Christ. Only

[32] Rt. Rev. Frank W. Creighton in *The Spirit of Missions*, November, 1934, p. 544.

the eyes which have been purified from selfishness and prejudice can perceive this. Only lips which are courageous will proclaim it. But the men who see it and proclaim it will be those who can help keep faith burning through apocalyptic crises and become the rallying points of a Church which will mean far more to the future than the Church is meaning now.

CHAPTER VII

WHEN THE NEW PROPHETS COME

AT the close of the preceding chapter, we were thinking of the Christian Church in its relation to
the life of the present day.

To the thought of many that relationship is no longer
the vital thing which once it was. There are some who
look upon the Church doubtfully, as some also who regard it with hostility and derision.

In the ranks of the doubters are many who would not
naturally be disaffected. Men and women may drift
away from interest in the Church without having lost
their interest in the realities which the Church is supposed to safeguard. The best of them want to be loyal
to the spirit of Christ. They believe that no influence
but his can lead our civilization out of its confusion
into a more abundant life. Moved by the compassion
which Christ has created in them, and led by ideals
which he somehow made so commanding that they
never can escape their power, they give their energy
to many kinds of unselfish work in settlements, in hospitals, in organized philanthropies innumerable. They
go out readily enough into the whole field of social
service; but the Church seems to them to have only a
faint relation to these things. The open doors through

which people go in to worship on Sunday do not seem to
them to lead out again into any connection with the
particular roads where they are walking. They may be
what Norman Thomas one day called those who now
are like himself—"wistful outsiders"; but they are
outsiders just the same.

Others, of course, are outside the Church with a more
definite repudiation. They look upon it with dislike.
To them it seems either a collection of little groups of
ineffective people, or else in its larger aspect an obscurantist drag upon the progress of man's life. They think
of the Church as it has been seen in Russia, tied to the
interests of an old regime, or stubbornly standing in the
way of change as it has stood in Spain, or fighting to
keep its old prerogatives as it does today in Mexico.
Or they see the Church, as sometimes a part of organized Protestantism has represented it in America, playing upon popular ignorance in the name of religion, as
with the Tennessee anti-evolutionary laws; or rousing
great legislative clamor against minor wickednesses,
while more grievous forms of social and economic in-
iquity go unrebuked.

This widespread criticism of the Church affects men
who might otherwise be inclined toward the ministry.
Some men even enter the seminaries who still are in
doubt as to whether they want to become pastors and
preachers to established congregations. They may go
off into by-ways of what they call religious education

conducted according to the project method, which sometimes is more project than it is either education or
religion. They may develop a fever of social experi-
mentation; and, with reforming zeal for institutions
concerning which somebody else is responsible, set out,
as one harassed but humorous president of a seminary
put it, "to turn these into guinea-pigs for the Soviet."
"The Lord hath chastened me sore; but he hath not given
me over unto death," [1] cried the psalmist of his Creator;
but a good many of the eager and earnest oncoming
generation are more radical when it comes to dealing
with the Church. They will both chasten and correct it;
and they are not sure that they will stop there. If
they allow the Church to escape being given over completely unto death, it may be after the manner of the
phœnix, rising perilously out of the flames of the funeral
pyre which they propose to light.

In short, there is abroad in many quarters today the
question as to whether organized Christianity in the
form in which we have known it ought to survive.
Granted that we need the values of the Kingdom of God
to be established in this world, may they perhaps be better served by some new instrumentality altogether? Is
the Church the torch-bearer of a creative truth, or is it
only a spent tradition?

Now every one will admit that the Church must plead

[1] Psalm 118:18.

guilty to some of the indictments brought against it. Those who see the Church's shortcomings are not only those who stand outside it. People who are inside have put up with a good deal more than the random critic knows about; but nevertheless they have no more lost their faith in the Church's greatness than men lose their faith in their home when its human complications give evidence that it is still this side of Paradise. Bishop Warburton back in eighteenth-century England expressed the fact in somewhat startling but effective language when he wrote: "The Church, like the ark, is worth saving, not for the unclean beasts and vermin who nearly filled it and made most of the noise and clamor, but for the little kernel of rationality who endured as best they might, and doubtless were more disturbed by the stink within than by the storm without." [2]

During the unpleasantly prolonged bad weather, the ark undoubtedly became exceedingly cramped and monotonous. Noah and his family could easily have imagined more desirable accommodations; but, nevertheless, it was due to the accommodations which they did have that when the rain stopped and the sun came out they were still alive and not drowned with their former neighbors. The earth for its new—and it was to be hoped its better—population had to depend on the little group who had stuck things through in the ark. The old story is a more living parable than some are inclined

[2] Quoted from memory; and unhappily I cannot find again the exact reference.—W. R. B.

to recognize. The spiritual ark of the Church, in spite of all that theoretical designers might object to in its limited dimensions, and sometimes its lack of ventilation, does hold within it the human spirits upon whom by and large the hope of better days depend. Everybody knows that when any good cause is launched in a community the first thing that its sponsors would like to get hold of is the list of the members of churches, for these people have consciences which at least are sensitive. They may be very average human beings; but they have the grace to know full well that through the woods and vales life is supposed to lead uphill. Measured by God's possibilities the Church may be pitiable, but the Church measured against other human institutions still can take the highest place. The average within it will be higher than the average without, both in desire and in deed.

And as men who understand the Church see this, they see something else also. They see not only the Church's actuality, but its ideal. Viewed in its externals, the Church does seem, as we have already said, to be made up of little congregations not severally impressive, or else brought together as an organized influence which too frequently is blundering and inept. But the seer of profounder things will know that the true Church is something far more beautiful. The Church as at any moment it exists is only the rude copying by human hands of a pattern never quite forgotten. It is the embryo which is as yet only a far-off approximation to that which is its inherent glory. For the Church is meant to be the Body of Christ. In its mystical fulfilment it must be the extension of his incarnation on this earth.

In all illumined moments of awareness men perceive this meaning of the Church. This is the fascination of the Catholic ideal, when that word is used not in any narrow or partisan sense, but as the expression of a dream that does bring the broken facts of existence into an immortal unity. The Church Catholic rises out of the confusion of the little lives which enter into it, and represents the dignity of soul which no single life attains but toward which the best in all is striving. In the presence of the great shrines which have gathered round themselves the spiritual history of the ages, one knows that this is true. Who can stand within the nave of Chartres and gaze upon the unearthly glory of its west windows and not feel there the ineffable poetry of the soul of man which will be living when the last sunset of recorded time has died into the dark? Who can go into the dim spaces of the Abbey of Westminster, particularly if for one hour of privilege he may be there alone, and conscious there of the awful fellowship of the illustrious dead, not realize anew that life and death are lifted into dignity only when they become part of the agelong pilgrimage of human souls that climb the ascending way to God? Before the witness of the continuity of the Church, all little separating things of name and nation melt away. The citizen of any country may be a citizen of the universal household of the faith, and all of hope and inspiration and patient brave desire which has belonged to any people belongs by right to him. From this land of ours in a certain year went a traveller on a pilgrimage to England, and of the moments there when the timeless voice of history seemed to speak to him he remembers particularly one. On a summer's night he stood in the garden of the deanery at York. Round him were the shadows of great, still trees; and behind him, forming two boundaries of the garden, rose the parapeted wall where once the guardians of the mediæval city kept their watch. In front of him, silhouetted against the sky that shimmered with the silver flame of a full moon, rose the majestic mass of the ancient minster. In the silence of the night its arches and its towers seemed to hold a deeper silence. In comparison with its immense and shadowy calm even the quiet moon seemed ephemeral. Presently the moon would move upon its way across the bridge of stars and dip below the horizon and be gone. And the one who stood there watching in the garden reflected upon how many moons had waxed and waned, and upon how many times the summer and the winter stars had climbed the sky in the centuries since that cathedral had been standing there. Across the deep-worn stones of its threshold had come kings and commoners, knights who would follow the road of far crusades and men and women whose steps would never range beyond the narrow streets of their own town. But all alike, the lowly and the great, the men of starry names and the men of names unknown, brought there to that cathedral the hunger of the heart for something infinite which they believed the Church would satisfy. And still the Church, the Church whose symbol may be the stones of ancient shrines, but the Church the spiritual reality of which is greater than any symbol, large or small, *this* Church exists to fascinate and command the instincts of the best of human kind.

It is a curious fact that in our generation when many people have been estranged from the Church altogether, many others have turned toward the Christian Church in those forms of it which are most definite and authoritarian. In England, men like Gilbert Chesterton and Alfred Noyes and Father Knox go into the Church of Rome. Within the Church of England there has been a reassertion of the emphasis of the Oxford Movement of an hundred years ago, and large numbers have been drawn into those Anglo-Catholic groups which lay stress upon what they believe to be the inheritance of the undivided Church, exalt the priesthood as the only ministry of a valid sacrament, and regard the Church as the custodian of a faith to which the individual must obediently conform. Similarly here in the United States the so-called Catholic movement in the Protestant Episcopal Church is strong. Moreover, a surprising number of ministers from other Protestant communions find themselves drawn into the Episcopal Church, and more frequently than not into that group within it which magnifies the authority of the ecclesiastical order most.

What are the reasons back of facts like these? They are many and various. But the reason which matters most, and the one which has in it an instinctive desire which illumines the significance of the Church is this: men and women want to feel that in the midst of their disturbed and uncertain world there is something sure. They want to be stayed not by something which they have to gain, but by that which is already given. They want to feel concerning the visible institution which represents God that which Clough sang of God the invisible:

> "It fortifies my soul to know
> That, though I perish, Truth is so;
> That, howsoe'er I stray and range,
> Whate'er I do, Thou dost not change.
> I steadier step when I recall
> That, if I slip, Thou dost not fall." [3]

This yearning for the benediction of the Church which represents not the ideas of the individual but the inheritance of the race sometimes may be made vivid by a single revealing incident and symbol. Once in the middle of the night an Episcopal clergyman was called to a hospital to be with one of his parishioners who was dying. Answering the call hastily, he went out

[3] From poem beginning "O Thou Whose Image," by Arthur Hugh Clough, in *Poems of Clough,* edited by H. S. Milford, p. 70.

leaving his Prayer Book behind. When he reached the hospital, the mother of the dying girl asked him to kneel down and have a prayer with her. He knelt and prayed a prayer which came from the reality of his sympathy and comradeship, a prayer of his own heart's cry on her behalf for the presence of God which they sought together. When he had finished, she thanked him; and then presently she asked him if he would also have the prayers from the Book of Common Prayer. He went home and got his book, for he understood what it was that she desired. She was not unappreciative of the prayer which he had offered. All the help that came through it she received, but she also wanted something else. In that deep moment of distress and darkness, she wanted to feel that the petitions to be uttered should not be those framed by any single lips, but those which came as it were with the voice of all the gathered centuries. She wanted to hear a note not of one man's faith, but of that faith which had been shaped through the long patience and the proved experience of the Church. She wanted to seek God not only along the way of any one individual's leading, but along the ways which had been lighted by the soul of man.

When any are tempted to depreciate the Church, let them remember what it is that men and women seek through all the broken and often pitiful expressions of God which organized religion may present. They are trying to feel again the meaning of the Incarnation, and to believe that there is on earth a body of experience through which the reality of God comes again to human need. And it does so come. Back of all the imperfections, and deeper than all the divisions of the Church, there is a grace which touches those who truly worship. People are made better in and through the Church, more sensitive, more kind, more gentle, more steadfast for the duties of the common day than otherwise they would have been. This is no small thing, even though the impatient propagandists of mass progress may forget it. In the long run, there can be no very noble society unless there are nobler people. Even the so-called atheistic social movements of our day have at the heart of them a profound religious impulse, an impulse that is an inheritance, though it be from afar-off, from the sort of religious consciousness which the Church has kept aflame all down the years. And if a better social order is to be achieved, it will certainly be achieved at less cost to whatever is beautiful in our present civilization, and will be more spiritually spacious when it comes, if the sort of religion which is cultivated in the churches has part in its determining. Nor is that all. Even if the most desirable new order which social reformers can imagine were ushered in, there would be no ultimate joy in it unless the human beings composing it should find what men and women all through the ages have been looking for when they turned toward the Church. They want a sense of infinity in the midst of time. They want bread for their souls and not only for their bodies. There is a part of their nature which could never be sheltered by the most modern housing. They need a temple of loftier thoughts and more mystic beliefs than any physical accommodations can provide. When all is said and done, the real values of life are in the quivering inner things, in beauty and passion, in love and loyalty, in great fulfilments and in the agony of great loss, in the far aims men can never quite master, and in the mystery of death. Who shall speak to them an authentic word concerning these? This is what they will forever ask— or begin again to ask after they have forgotten—and that is why organized religion will never be uprooted from this earth.

Let no man think, then, that if he ministers faithfully to a congregation of average men and women who represent among themselves our human nature's ordinary needs he is doing a small and insignificant thing. He may be helping to keep alive those values out of which all that is transcendent in our ultimate human destiny must be born. A very gentle and brave spirit, old Bishop Randolph of Southern Virginia, spoke once to his clergy these words which reveal the singularly penetrating and winsome quality of his own preaching. "When you preach," he said, "you must think of your

people as they have been revealed to you in the close
relation of pastor and flock. Think of youth with its
joyous strength, of men and women out in the battle of
life, tempted and fighting with temptation. How wonderful would your congregation be to you if you could
see underneath the surface as they sit before you on
Sunday morning. Yonder, perchance, is the bride with
the orange blossoms hardly faded, and yonder the
mother, who, while you are preaching of the love of
God, is looking away toward the city of the dead and
thinking of the green grave of her child whom God
has taken. Yonder is tempted manhood shadowed by
some lust of the flesh or sophistry of the devil, or
yonder again is the complacent worldling who wonders
why these Christian people call themselves 'miserable
sinners.' He thinks in his inward heart that it is all
unmeaning formality. He repudiates the great Christian confession of sin. He repudiates the need of the
Christian redemption and of the Saviour's Cross. To all
these varied types of character and condition, and of
experience, to all of these throbbing hearts you are to
preach—Christ, and Him crucified. You must think
of them all in the vision when you are getting ready to
preach, and then you must get down on your knees
and ask Christ to help you. You are responsible to Him,
and in a strange wonderful sense, He is responsible to
you. He called you to go forth and preach His Gospel,

and with the command He gives the promise every Sunday, 'I will be with you to the end of the world.' " [4]

Thus far we have thought of the Church in a way which would satisfy many of the defenders of the ecclesiastical *status quo*. "This is what we have always said," they would declare. "We have said that the Church has a message which the world needs to listen to instead of going off on its own wild ways of newness. If men would enter the Church and be saved into a different sort of spiritual condition, then social improvements and reformations would take care of themselves. It is not conditions that count, but character. Let people come to Christ, and everything else desirable will then come to them." Many ecclesiastics have spoken in that fashion, and the hidden harm in what they have said has affected equally those who believed them and those who did not believe. For many who believe have been led to think of the Church as a static thing, and to suppose that if they kept repeating the religious experiences of yesterday, this is all that life needs. And those who did not believe them, seeing that the Church often did become static and self-centered, have supposed that, no matter what might be the theoretical values of organized religion, it had to be got rid of because it stood in the way of human progress.

[4] *Annual Address to Council of the Diocese of Southern Virginia, 1912.*

The fact is that two values are involved, and this always makes a tension. The impatient spirit tries to get rid of tension by denying one influence in favor of the other; but the greatness of life requires that we go on trying to hold in balance the two opposing poles between which the full truth turns. In regard to the Church, we must believe, on the one hand, that it preserves the convictions which are timeless; and on the other hand, we must know that these convictions must show their validity in relation to new facts and new times if they are to retain significance.

Now the error among many churchmen, and especially among those who like to glory in what they call their Catholic heritage, is that they think of faith as something finished and not as something infinitely fertile. They tend to make the authority of the Church rest on title-deeds rather than on the test of living demonstration. They rightly insist on the weight of those beliefs which are historic; but they often forget that history is no closed book, but is a continuous reality in which neither the past nor the present can be truly interpreted alone. The ultra-conservative Catholic is as a scientist would be if that scientist lacked the everlasting humility of open-mindedness which makes the real scientist what he is. The Catholic may be impatient of new factors entering into his problem out of the endless spontaneity of life. He wants to close his hypotheses and have a summing up of truth which is concluded once for all.

One may see this in the instinctive approach which many ecclesiastics make to that large effort in the direction of Christian unity called *The World Conference on Faith and Order*. In that title, what does *Faith* and what does *Order* mean? Faith is a thing "once delivered to the saints." To the conventionally-minded churchman, it means a deposit of beliefs crystallized long ago. It is the body of dogma made by men now dead to which living men must subscribe, and neither one jot nor one tittle must pass away from that enduring law. The look of men who conceive faith in this fashion is always turning backward. They want to establish what the early Church Fathers said or what the Council of Nicæa or Ephesus or Chalcedon decreed. If they can establish this, then they think they have set the boundaries beyond which no proper and orthodox thinking must pass. If the Church was thus and thus in the sacrosanct yesterdays, then thus it must remain.

And what, in the thought of these same men, is *Order?* It is the fixed constitution of Church government and ministry. It is the form supposed not only to have been established and stereotyped by antiquity, but to have been ordained by Christ himself, which the ministry or the priesthood of the Church is to retain if it is to be spiritually valid. Men who hold the rigid position which goes by the name "Catholic," whether they be Roman or Anglican, are alike in their fundamental supposition. They differ in their claim as to what the *Order* is, but each is equally sure that there is an *Order,* and that *he* knows it and *he* has it. From that framework of Church regularity, he thinks he has no business to deviate. He may be full of gracious personal consideration for other Christians, but officially he will say that he has no right to endanger the *Order* which he believes has come down from Christ. If the *Order* were admitted to be questionable, if the authority of the Pope, or the Apostolic Succession of Bishops, or the Divine Right of the Priesthood were admitted to be debatable, then the whole Christian structure would collapse.

Now, of course, the whole fact of life denies that. "The Spirit bloweth where it listeth," and breathes upon men in many ways. It is not subject to control by any ecclesiastical routine. Christ embodies himself and conveys his grace among many different sorts of Christians. And when men venture out beyond the jealous fences of their theories and look at truth, they know it.

· What is needed in the Church of today and tomorrow is a leadership which sees the right relation between the Church's inheritance and the Church's task. Its inheritance is authoritative just in so far as it can be translated into the living task. If it be seen that such and such an expression of the *Faith* and such and such an ecclesiastical *Order* do actually create a Church more coherent, more eager and more effective for the work of Christ, then these will prevail by their own self-evidencing worth. To treat flippantly the presumptions created by long history is foolish; but to insist that what has been can never be changed into a larger synthesis is to deny the continuing reality of the Holy Spirit. If the theologians of the great Councils should speak today, or the early Fathers of the Church, or the Apostles, would they not in their ripened understanding say to us that if the Church is to be indeed the continuing incarnation of the influence of Christ, it must be such not by insisting dogmatically upon the exact measurements which the body has had before, but by giving free course to his life which re-creates the body according to the new environment in which it functions? Nor could the truth which ought to come down through the Church from the great forerunners to their successors be more nobly expressed than in these words which a modern servant of mankind, Octavia Hill, of London, wrote for those who took up the work of betterment for the poor which she had begun: "When I am gone, I hope my friends will not try to carry out any special system, or to follow blindly in the track which I have trodden. New circumstances require various efforts; and it is the spirit, not the dead form, that should be perpetuated. When the time comes that we slip from our places, and they are called to the front as leaders, what should they inherit from us? Not a system, not an association, not dead formulas. . . . What we care most to leave them is not any tangible thing, however great, not any memory, however good, but the quick eye to see, the true soul to measure, the large hope to grasp the mighty issues of the new and better days to come—greater ideals, greater hope, and patience to realise both." [5]

"Greater ideals, greater hope, and patience to realise both"—these are the objectives which the Church must take in this present time. Not the old ideals only, nor the old hope, but something bolder. It is not enough to produce a spiritual leaven within a limited group. It is not enough to preserve an ecclesiastical organization, no matter how orthodox and correct. The test of the validity of the Church today will be whether or not it can contribute an effective influence to the building of a society which in its social, economic, and international relationships shall represent those values in human life for which Christ lived and died.

Let none who love the Church fail to appreciate the critical reality of the judgment which is upon her now. It is not too much to say that the next half-century may reveal whether or not the Church deserves to endure, or whether or not as an institution it will crumble and the spirit of Christ embody itself in some other form.

[5] *Life of Octavia Hill,* by C. Edmund Maurice, p. 582.

In a book which Raymond Robbins wrote concerning Russia shortly after the downfall of the old régime and the outbreak of the revolution, he used by way of illustration one unforgetable phrase. He described how the privileged class in Russia had gone the round of their isolated and self-sufficient life, in sheltered wealth and careless gaiety, with the silken curtains drawn across windows through which they did not see the ominous forces moving in the dark night of the common life of Russia. They had, he said, *the indoor mind.* Their thoughts and imagination did not go out into the terrible open spaces where the new forces of change were gathering. There is danger today that the Church may have "the indoor mind." It may be stodgy, blind, complacent. There are great numbers of lay people who have not waked up to the fact that the Church ought to have a dynamic relationship to the issues which affect all the people. They want to keep it decorous and aloof. They are far more concerned lest their particular parish should be involved in anything which they call a sensation than they are that it should be a spiritual force Ministers and preachers may succumb to this slowly stifling mood. They too may think that they have done enough when they have kept the ecclesiastical light burning within the little shelter of their affairs. But it is not so. The world at large has at least a dim awareness that the Church possesses in itself great unused resources which ought to be available for a better world.

They know that the Church claims to worship Jesus, who loved the common people. They know it affirms the pre-eminence of personality. They know it preaches brotherhood. They know it proclaims that love can do more for human beings than selfishness and violence. And they are looking to see whether there will be any sweep of courage and any reckless daring in the Church. Bishop Charles H. Brent said once: "I may be a fool; but if so I will be God's fool." With that same reliance upon a heavenly fact, the Church must reflect a foolishness of God which in the long run is the only wisdom. It must prove in the face of all the stubborn contradictions of this age that the spirit of Christ crucified is at last not a dream and not a tragic gesture, but the wisdom of God and the *power* of God.

The air is full today of prophecies of inevitable revolution and of the kind of revolution which will drown many of man's spiritual hopes in blood. Many men, even Christian teachers like Reinhold Niebuhr, believe that there is no other way by which a better society can be at last achieved beyond the long confusion into which our civilization now is sinking. But neither blind revolution nor catastrophe ought to be inevitable. To say that they are is to quench the light of that indomitable faith which the prophets have always kept burning through every darkest night. The Church must not believe that disaster is inevitable. But it must believe, and must proclaim, that disaster is inevitable, *unless*——

Unless men see in time the awful realities of judgment written upon the structure of our civilization, like the *Mene, Mene, Tekel, Upharsin* written by the moving fingers upon Belshazzar's wall. The prophet of God who goes into a Christian pulpit must know that he stands today, as his Master stood, in the midst of a wicked and adulterous generation. Of that generation he himself is part; so he will preach to it from no aloof and self-righteous superiority. He must try to be to it its own conscience made articulate, so that men and women underneath their outward respectability may recognize the grievous adulteries of spirit by which society has been married to the unclean seductions of greed and ruthless power. They must be helped to see that God is not mocked; and that whatsoever a generation soweth that shall it also reap. They must be made to understand that history marches upon an inexorable way; and that there are forces of retribution which once they have been set in motion, will not be turned aside until men are ready to pay the cost of great repentance.

The true prophets of God, preaching truth to a world that wanted to be undisturbed, have never been popular. It is a hard thing for an individual, or for a people, to face the costly implications of those ideals which they dare not deny but which they would fain forget. The preacher is tempted to speak the smooth vaguenesses which his listeners prefer to hear. But there have always been men, and there must be men now, who will not do that. The pioneers among the prophets set an example which never can be lost. Elijah confronted Ahab at the gate of Naboth's vineyard which Ahab had wickedly possessed. Amos set forth the facts of his time with a plainness which no one could misunderstand. He spoke of those who "sold the righteous for silver, and the poor for a pair of shoes." [6] He spoke of those who "store up violence and robbery in their palaces," [7] who afflict the just, take bribes, and turn the poor aside from their right. For these reasons, he said, judgment should come upon the nation; for these iniquities no amount of ostentatious religion could be a shield. "Let judgment run down as waters," he said, "and righteousness as a mighty stream." [8]

Here in America, in the decade which led up to this present period of depression and disillusionment, there were spokesmen of religion who to the best of their ability pointed out the evils in this our own society which cried out for correction. Individuals and church assemblies condemned the brutal selfishness of child labor, assailed the intolerably long hours which many factories and foundries forced their men to work, pointed out the industrial hazards which claimed their great toll of deaths and maimings every year, and showed the starvation wages which some industries, on the plea of business necessity, were forcing their la-

[6] Amos 2:6.　　　[7] Amos 3:10.　　　[8] Amos 5:24.

borers to accept. We have been driven now to the huge
and costly belated attempt to remedy these injustices,
when we might have remedied them long ago if our
national conscience had been more enlightened; but the
plain fact is that they have got to be remedied, and
other and deeper evils bound up with the whole accepted
profit-motive in our economic organization will have to
be remedied if we are to escape the doom of a growing
bitterness and collision. If we fail to understand this
and to heed it, the prophecy may be brought to us which
Amos brought to Israel, the prophecy of a day when it
shall be "As if a man did flee from a lion, and a bear
met him; or went into the house, and leaned his hand
on the wall, and a serpent bit him. Shall not the day of
the Lord be darkness, and not light? Even very dark,
and no brightness in it?" [9]

It is a wholesome thing that we should remember
how many civilizations which thought themselves great
upon this earth have gone on their descending way, and
at last have disappeared. Every civilization pretends to
think that it is invulnerable, and we in America are no
exception to that rule. We glibly assume that we are in
some special way the favored people of the Almighty.
Other societies may disintegrate, but not ours. But any
such boast, even by the mightiest of peoples, sounds hollow before the silent scorn of the inexorable centuries.
Is it likely that Egypt, when her pharaohs built their

[9] Amos 5:19, 20.

pyramids, ever thought that those pyramids would look back to an empire which had scarcely left its foot-prints in the desert sand? Is it likely that Babylonia and Assyria, when their iron chariots rolled like waves of the sea across a conquered shore, ever dreamed that Babylon and Nineveh, with a splendor which then amazed the world, would ultimately be only dust-heaps where the jackals prowled? Did Rome of the Cæsars dream that it would sink for ages into ruin? Or did Philip the Second ever imagine that the time would come when all the galleons of Spain would vanish from the sea?

We know they did not think so, and neither is it easy for men in America today to think that this huge structure of civilization which we have reared in the western world should ever be seriously endangered. But if we are wise we shall remember that the people which has great privileges from God will be held to a great accountability. Though the mills of God grind slowly, yet they grind exceeding small; and in the long run, if this nation is to remain great, it can do so only by a moral stamina which shall make it deserve enduring greatness.

But the prophet and preacher who points out the social sins which cry for repentance (sins, let it be remembered always, which belong not only to others but also to *him*) must not stultify his preaching by the dour assumption that the repentance he pleads for will not come. In Sargent's great frieze of the prophets, in the

Boston Public Library, some of them sit upon the ground with bowed shoulders and ashes upon their heads; but the greater figures stand erect with arms uplifted and the light of the far vision kindling in their transfigured eyes. Because they trusted invincibly in God, they could never wholly despair of men. And so it should be now. It is not true that our social order must drift into blind and brutal chaos. There is yet time for the spread of a spirit which can so reduce resistance to the demand of social change, because men confess great changes to be just, that the larger good of all may gradually be worked out together. There is yet time for the vindication of what the fashion of our age derides—the *liberal* gospel. For a liberal gospel is built upon the belief that there is a height to which men can be lifted where they are free to see life in its larger reaches; and that the consecrated sanity of this far outlook may at last assume direction of those instinctive passions which move men in the mass. Let no Christian preacher today abandon this great hope, for if he does, then he will have lost the glory of the accolade of Christ!

The correction of our industrial and economic evils is tied up with another great menace of our time, namely, the fateful possibility of war. Unintelligent greed pressing for unlimited material opportunity, the drive of capitalistic production to secure markets for its products, the exploitation of weak people by the strong

—these things, together with the artificially excited pride and prejudice of race, set the drums beating for those wild outbursts of national hysteria which not only kill human bodies but corrupt human souls. The war against war must be directed both against the long range causes and against the threatening fact. The Christian message must show the economic chain of cause and effect which must be broken or redirected. It must stand —as with magnificent heroism the Protestant minorities have stood in Nazi Germany—against a nationalism gone mad. And in the end it may have to stand against war by deliberately setting Christ above Cæsar, and taking the consequences of that allegiance.

For let it not be forgotten that always in the Christian gospel there is the looming possibility of the cross. Christians are to believe in and to preach the supreme worth of personality, and the costly implications of Christ's law of love; and they are to trust that these will lead our world on paths of peace. But they cannot be blind to the dark forces which a sluggish Christianity too long has suffered to gather. It may be true that those who shall dare to speak and act as Christians may have to be crucified between the colliding passions of Communism and Fascism; and that failing to bring in a better present social order, they may only become the seed for some far-off consummation watered now by blood and tears. It may be that Christians in any and every nation cannot prevent another war (although it may be also that they can!) ; and if not, then it will not be the first time that Christians have been given to the lions. It has often been thought that the world might be saved from wars by majority opinion. It has been thought that it might be saved by the common sense of all the peoples expressed through the reasonable and patient policies of their governments. It has been thought that it might be saved by the League of Nations and the World Court. But none of these may be enough. There may need to be poured into the crucible out of which, please God, some day the gold of our redemption may be refined, another and a costlier element. There must be the dedication, and perhaps the sacrifice, of men and women in every country who are bound together by a new covenant which God has written in their hearts, a covenant which is not contrary to their love of country but which includes it, a covenant of men and women who believe that in the long run there is a redeeming loyalty to nation and to flag which can be found only when people in every land are loyal first to God. In other words, we need the company of men and women in all nations who believe that wars can be ended only as there are in all countries a growing number who will say that in all foreseeable circumstances and at all costs they will resist war. That will not be easy. It will involve, if war does come, a breach between the Church and the majority of the nation. It will involve, for those who dare to take this stand and to maintain it, a storm of criticism and of hatred, loss of position, punishment, imprisonment, violence. But only through such costly influences as these are the forces of this world's real redemption set on foot. And for the Church there could be no greater privilege than that it espouse a cause so great and so sacrificial that it should begin once again to be worthy of him who set his face toward a cross. The real peril of the Church today lies not in its doing a perilous thing but in its drifting on in a kind of conformity to the world which has no peril in it. There is not much in our ecclesiastical life which appeals to moral heroism; but a Church here in America, in England, in Germany, in Japan, which sets itself against war, a Church within the Church which is stronger than the barriers of nation and of race, will have room for moral heroes. It is time for such a Church to arise— and for men to arise who dare to be its preachers.

As this more daring and adventurous day draws near, the men who stand in Christian pulpits may well thank God and be glad. The best men will not be drawn into the Church in days of safety. They will be drawn when there is something noble and worth while to risk. E. Stanley Jones has symbolized a great truth in one of the paragraphs of *The Christ of Every Road*. "In Valparaiso, which means 'the Vale of Paradise,' I saw the beautiful harbor strewn with the hulks of wrecked ships. I wondered why there was so much wreckage in this Vale of Paradise. I was told that the harbor though beautiful is subject to terrific storms which break in from the sea, and that the only safe thing to do in a storm is to weigh anchor and make for the open ocean. Ships that hug the safety of the harbor are almost invariably wrecked. . . . If religion hugs its safe harbors and gazes upon its entrancing vales of paradise, the wreckage of the future will be terrible. . . . The only safety is in the open sea." [10]

That is to say, safety is in the bold adventure—not the mean safety of avoidance, but the safety of a great hazard carried through to far success. The man who dares in this our time to be an interpreter of truth for the Christian Church must be both an adventurer and an explorer. He must follow the gleams of what seem to him reality, though they may lead on ways that tax his utmost thought and demand an unflagging courage. Often it will be true of him, as in the magnificent symbolic words that were written concerning Abraham who being "called to go out into a place which he after should receive for an inheritance, obeyed; and he went out, not knowing whither he went." [11] The preacher who seeks to find God's message for his generation starts on a quest, and that quest is unfinished to his life's end. He is like a pilgrim who never fully reaches his goal, but

[10] P. 32. Copyright, 1930. By permission of the Abingdon Press.
[11] Hebrews 11 :8.

always sees it shining at the end of a longer way. He goes out, and in the sense of an altogether completed task, he is never to come in.

Those souls in every generation who have in them any quality of the spiritual prophet and pioneer know what this means. Like Abraham, they have not been able to rest in the narrow and complacent conditions to which they were born. They seek a more heavenly country somewhere on this earth. They want to find and to create a life more true, more righteous, more beautiful than that with which most of their neighbors are content. They want more generous relationships among individuals. They want a social and economic order which is more just and kind. They want to see old, narrow nationalisms melt into a new unity of the nations. They want to see the pitiful divisions of our several Churches broken down in the new inclusiveness of a great Church obedient to the living will of God. But the ideal is seldom or never realized in their day. They are pilgrims and sojourners on the fields of their devotion. Like Abraham they dwell in tents, establishing their venture here today, moving on to something else tomorrow, never reaching that which they could rest in as their final vindication.

Ordinary men, looking at them, think that they have failed. The world usually thinks that the pioneers of its own generation have failed, for the world wants results, and the results which pioneers have desired are a long time coming. Joan of Arc, who followed her voices to deliver France, died at the stake in the market-place of Rouen, and France was not yet free. Savonarola, prophet of a new moral reformation in the corrupt last days of the mediæval Church, was burned in Florence, and the city which he died for seemed as wicked as it had ever been. William Tyndale, who brought the Bible to the English people in their own tongue, had his body brutally dishonored and his ashes thrown into the sea. John Bunyan, whose soul was bright with the vision of *Pilgrim's Progress,* was kept for twelve years in Bedford jail. William Wilberforce and Lord Shaftesbury, who fought to overthrow chattel slavery and the scarcely less cruel industrial slavery which blackened the early nineteenth century England, were regarded with hatred by many of their own social class. The men and women in the nineteenth century and in the early twentieth who have gone ahead of the crowd in new programs of social justice or of international co-operation for world peace have had to endure the crowd's rejection. The stodgy men, the safe and sane men, the men who always want to keep their world as they found it, because it is more familiar and more comfortable thus, can never appreciate the pioneer. They do not believe in his success because to them success must be measured by the here and now. They do not understand the kind of spiritual victory whose fulfilment will be tomorrow, but not today.

But the man who has in his soul some spark of the pioneer goes on. It does not dismay him if he cannot do all that he would like to do. It does not dismay him if the ideals he believes in and proclaims, ideals for private life and for public life, are flouted and postponed. He knows that any man who sets out to be in the advance guard for human opinion and human choice has adventured upon a long road. He does not need to have assurance of quick results if only he is satisfied that his direction is right. He does not have to know altogether where his path leads if he knows why it leads. He does not have to perceive the end from the beginning if only he is confident that beside him and above him is the reality of God, who sees what he cannot see. It is enough that he hears a voice telling him to go forward and to keep on, for in his heart is sounding the divine assurance, *"I* am the beginning and the end." [12]

Yet sometimes, of course, there may come the moods of discouragement and of near dismay. The goal of any adequate translation of the Christian ideal into life seems so remote and the difficulties in the way so great that Christian men, in preaching and in practice, may wonder whether they can keep faith burning and carry through till the great objective of the kingdom of Christ's Spirit comes in sight. In such times, let them remember that the way of the spiritual explorer and pioneer is glorious because of its very hardships and

[12] Revelation 22:13.

because of the heroic fortitude for which it calls. Well may they take upon their lips these words with which Admiral Peary, as he set out on the final journey which was at length to culminate in the conquest of the Pole, summed up his hope and faith. "Through all the seasons of disappointment and defeat I had never ceased to believe that the great white mystery of the North must eventually succumb to the insistence of human experience and will, and, standing there with my back to the world and my face toward that mystery, I believed that I should win in spite of all the powers of darkness and of desolation." [13]

In such a spirit men can preach and proclaim the heroic hazard of the gospel. The quest of Christian thought and will is for something farther and harder than the Pole. It is a search not for some spot upon this physical globe. It is a spiritual effort to perceive and to possess the new earth whereon dwelleth righteousness. It is an exploration toward "a city which hath foundations, whose builder and maker is God." [14] And notwithstanding much that always will be mystery, notwithstanding that from our world the darkness does not always smoothly pass away, those men of the Christian pulpits who would be God's explorers can turn their faces toward the great adventure and go forward unafraid.

[13] *The North Pole,* by Robert E. Peary, p. 41.
[14] Hebrews 11 :10.

INDEX

Acts 26 : 19, 160
Acts 19 : 13, 228
Adams, Henry, 45, 46
Addams, Jane, 118
American civilization, 281–283
Amos 2 : 6, 280
Amos 3 : 10, 280
Amos 5 : 24, 280
Amos 5 : 19, 20, 281
Athanasian Creed, 88
Atonement, doctrine of, 99–104
Authority for the Christian, 54–64

Babcock, Maltbie D., 107
Babylon, Assyria and Nineveh, 282
Barth, Karl, 220, 221
Beauty and recognition of God, 144–155
Bell, Bernard Iddings, 241
Bell, W. Cosby, 193, 194
Belshazzar's Wall, writing on, 279
Berdyaev, Nicholas, 233, 234
Book of Common Prayer, 107
Book of Common Prayer of the Church of England, 88
Bradford, Gamaliel, 45, 46
Brent, Charles H., 278
Brooks, Phillips, 6, 7, 12
Brown, William Adams, 141
Brunner, Emil, 220
Bunyan, John, 289
Bushnell, Horace, 12

Cabell, James Branch, 42
Cabot, Richard C., 68
Calvary, 104
Caruso, 21
Catholic conception of the church, 262–274
Catholic Encyclopædia, 93
Century Dictionary, 54
Chalcedonian Formula, 87
Chesterton, Gilbert, 65
Christians, authority for, not dogmatism, but discovery, 54–60; is based not on finality but on fertility, 64–68; the test of, 90

Christian Church, its relation to life of present day, 240–256; criticism of, 258–262; its ideal, 262–271; the two values involved, 272–281
Christian Communions in America, joint appeal of thirty national, 249, 250
Climate of religious confidence, 217–225
Clough, Arthur Hugh, 266
Coffin, Henry Sloane, 14, 113
Communion, Sacrament of, 104
Communism, 284
Compton, Arthur H., 153
Confessional Synod in Germany, recent manifesto of, 231, 232
Congregational Churches in United States, recent statement of, 250, 251
I Corinthians 9 : 16, 73
I Corinthians 1 : 20, 27, 191
I Corinthians 13 : 1, 248
II Corinthians 5 : 19, 61
II Corinthians 5 : 14, 73, 74
Couchoud, P. L., 76
Creeds, 87, 88, 90
Creighton, Frank W., 255, 256
Crothers, Samuel McChord, 7
Curie, Pierre and Marie, 119

Darrow, Clarence, 44
Darwin, 170
Day, Albert Edward, 27, 28
Discovery, the beginning of all dogma, 54–64
Dogma as defined in *Century Dictionary*, 54
Dreiser, Theodore, 42, 75
Drews, Arthur, 75

Easton, Burton S., 139
Economic measures of United States in recent crisis, 31, 32
Eliot, George, 5
Eliot, T. S., 47, 56

INDEX

nature, 168–169; and against depreciation of human personality, 169–173, 194–212; his correction of our materialistic estimate of success, 173–177, 212–216; effect of, 201–205; judgment of, 205–208; the freedom he gives, 210–211

Joan of Arc, 289

Job 11 : 7, 56

John 1 : 1, 86

John 12 : 21, 90

John 14 : 9, 90

John 14 : 21, 90

John 20 : 29, 107

John 14 : 28, 121

John 8 : 11, 207

John 16 : 33, 242

I John 4 : 19, 166

John the Baptist, 20–22

Johnson, F. Ernest, 252, 253

Jones, E. Stanley, 234, 235, 286, 287

Joseph, the story of, 158, 159

Jewish Rabbis, Conference of, 249

Jude 3 : 67, 91

Jung, C. C., 28, 29

Kingdom of God, 131–134, 240–243

Kirk, H. E., 19

Kirkland, Winifred, 79

Labouchère, Henri, 119

Lane, Franklin K., 40

Lawrence, Brother, 225

League of Nations, 285

Leibnitz, 217

Leiper, Henry Smith, 232

Lenin, 215

Leuba, James H., 180–184

Lewis, Sinclair, 42

Liberalism, 57–59, 243

Lindbergh, Charles A., 172

Liverpool Cathedral, Dean of, 88

Livingstone, David, 7

Luke 2 : 49, 131

Luke 23 : 43, 139

Luke 23 : 46, 139

Luther, Martin, 12, 36, 37, 62, 160

Macedonius, 19

Machen, J. Gresham, 56, 94

Mallory, George, 168

Man and the Spirit of Christ, 167–216

Mark 8 : 29, 86

Mark 1 : 31, 117

Mark 10 : 43, 118

Mark 10 : 18, 121

Mark 15 : 34, 138

Mark 8 : 33, 207

Mark 12 : 37, 200

Mary and Martha, 117

Matthew 4 : 4, 46

Matthew 11 : 25, 179

Matthew 10 : 34, 205

Matthew 20 : 27, 213

Meaning, search for and awareness of God, 148–155

Mencken, H. L., 42

Mercier, Joseph Désiré, 72, 140, 141, 161, 162

Mexico, Christian Church in, 254–256

Minister, larger name by which preacher may be called, 14; his friendship and service, 15–17

Miracles, 136, 137

Moses, 159, 160

Murry, Middleton, 128, 129, 138–140

Mussolini, Benito, 215

Myers, Frederic W. H., 53

Nehemiah 6 : 3, 160

Nicene Creed, 87, 88, 90

Niebuhr, Reinhold, 26, 222, 223

Nietzsche, Friedrich, 123, 239

Noyes, Alfred, 56

Osborne, Thomas Mott, 118

Otto, Rudolf, 53

Paul, 11, 12, 85, 160

Peary, Robert E., 291

Personality, reverence for, 230–240

Peter, 86

Philip the Second, 282

Pilgrim's Progress, 289

Pope Pius the Eleventh, 249

Power of passionate conviction, 215, 216

Preacher, an individual commissioned to particular task, 3–9;

Date Due